GREAT AMERICANS
A PHOTOBIOGRAPHY

HARRY S. TRUMAN

IDEALS PUBLICATIONS INCORPORATED

NASHVILLE, TENNESSEE

COVER PHOTO: Harry S. Truman, August 1944. Photo courtesy Harry S. Truman Library

Editor, Nancy J. Skarmeas; Copy Editor, Michelle Prater Burke; Designer, Anne C. Lesemann; Electronic Prepress, Tina Wells Davenport

Prepress by Precision Color Graphics, New Berlin, Wisconsin

Published by Ideals Publications Incorporated
535 Metroplex Drive, Suite 250
Nashville, Tennessee 37211

Printed and bound in Mexico by RR Donnelley & Sons

ISBN 0-8249-4078-4

First Edition
10 8 6 4 2 1 3 5 7 9

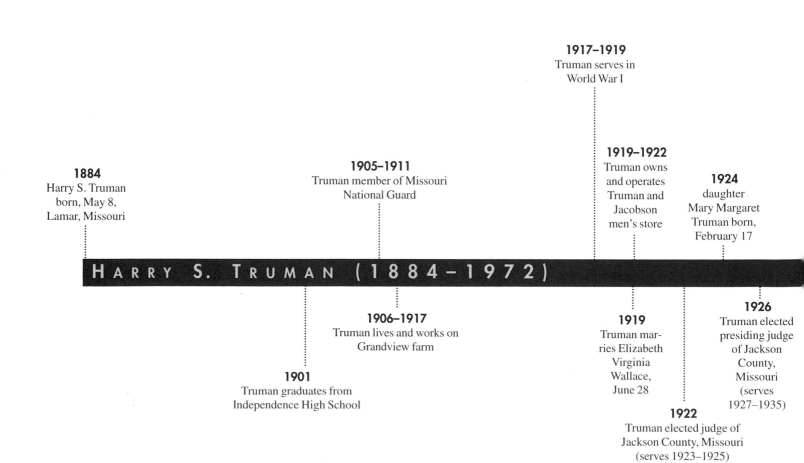

1917–1919
Truman serves in
World War I

1919–1922
Truman owns
and operates
Truman and
Jacobson
men's store

1924
daughter
Mary Margaret
Truman born,
February 17

1884
Harry S. Truman
born, May 8,
Lamar, Missouri

1905–1911
Truman member of Missouri
National Guard

HARRY S. TRUMAN (1884–1972)

1906–1917
Truman lives and works on
Grandview farm

1919
Truman mar-
ries Elizabeth
Virginia
Wallace,
June 28

1926
Truman elected
presiding judge
of Jackson
County,
Missouri
(serves
1927–1935)

1901
Truman graduates from
Independence High School

1922
Truman elected judge of
Jackson County, Missouri
(serves 1923–1925)

P R E F A C E

A great politician," Harry Truman wrote in 1954, "is known by the service he renders." Yet service alone cannot make a leader truly great. It was character that set Harry Truman apart. Born in the nineteenth century in Missouri, descended from pioneers and farmers, Truman was a man of unquestioned honor and integrity. In eight years as president, he faced some of the most difficult decisions ever to confront an American chief executive—decisions about world war, atomic weapons, and the spread of communism that affected not just the citizens of his own country but the population of the world. With a rare balance of humility and self-confidence, Truman put principle before politics; neither public opinion nor political expedience could sway him from a decision he believed was right. Many Americans were reluctant to accept that this inexperienced, unpolished man from Missouri could lead their nation, but Truman proved over and again an able, courageous, and incorruptible president.

A lifelong student of the past, Harry Truman liked to say that the only thing new is history we have yet to learn. For inspiration and guidance, he studied the lives of the great politicians and statesmen of the past; for posterity, he carefully preserved his letters, his personal memoranda, and his diary; and he worked diligently on his memoirs and his presidential library. For the biographer of Harry Truman, then, the challenge is not in discovering material, but in selecting from the wealth that is available. What follows is a collection of photos of Harry Truman and his times, accompanied by words from Truman's own pen: a photobiography of the plainspoken man from Missouri who helped shape the course of twentieth-century world history.

Harry Truman was the embodiment of the American belief that any child can grow up to be president. A man of humble origins, a farmer and a soldier, Truman knew life the way most ordinary Americans of his generation knew it, yet he made of his life something truly extraordinary. His story, so much of which is the story of the great events of the twentieth century, is both an inspiration and an education.

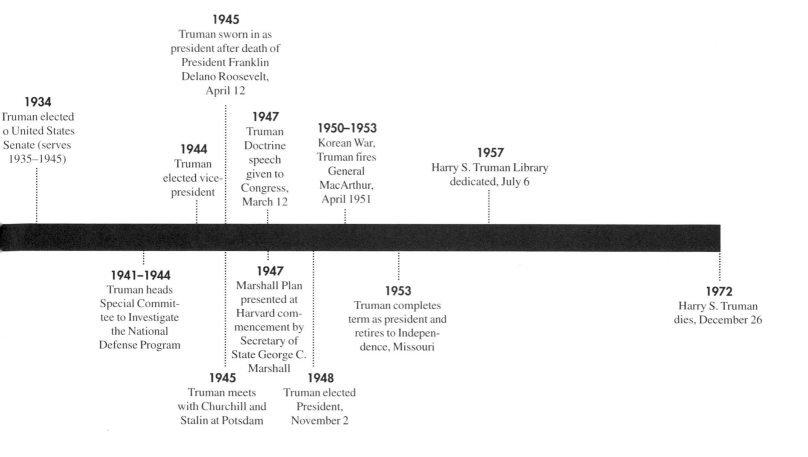

1945
Truman sworn in as president after death of President Franklin Delano Roosevelt, April 12

1934
Truman elected to United States Senate (serves 1935–1945)

1944
Truman elected vice-president

1947
Truman Doctrine speech given to Congress, March 12

1950–1953
Korean War, Truman fires General MacArthur, April 1951

1957
Harry S. Truman Library dedicated, July 6

1941–1944
Truman heads Special Committee to Investigate the National Defense Program

1947
Marshall Plan presented at Harvard commencement by Secretary of State George C. Marshall

1953
Truman completes term as president and retires to Independence, Missouri

1972
Harry S. Truman dies, December 26

1945
Truman meets with Churchill and Stalin at Potsdam

1948
Truman elected President, November 2

THE HAPPIEST CHILDHOOD

BY HARRY S. TRUMAN

Harry S. Truman was born on May 8, 1884, in his family's home in Lamar, Missouri. His first name was given in honor of his Uncle Harrison; his middle initial was a compromise tribute to both his maternal grandfather, Solomon Young, and his paternal grandfather, Anderson Shippe Truman. ABOVE RIGHT: Harry S. Truman in 1884, the first year of his life. Harry was the first child born to John and Martha Truman. He was followed by a brother, Vivian, and a sister, Mary Jane. Photo courtesy Harry S. Truman Library. All four of Truman's grandparents were pioneers who migrated to Missouri from Kentucky in the 1840s in search of fertile farmland. Truman's father, John Anderson Truman, was a self-educated farmer and horse trader with a reputation for unfailing honesty. His mother, Martha Young Truman, was a college-educated woman of unshakable principles. The Trumans raised their son to work hard, to be humble, and to tell the truth. BELOW RIGHT: Harry Truman's parents on their wedding day, 1881. Photo courtesy Harry S. Truman Library

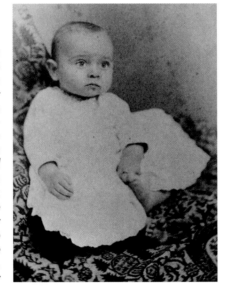

I was born in Lamar, Missouri, at four o'clock in the afternoon on May 8, 1884. When I was about a year old, the family moved to Cass County, Missouri, south of Harrisonville, where my father ran a farm and where my brother Vivian was born on April 25, 1886. In 1887 we moved to the Sol Young farm in Jackson County, two miles south of Hickman's Mill and six miles north of Belton in Cass County. . . . It was named Grandview because it was on a high point of land, the highest point in the vicinity. . . .

We had the whole 440 acres to play over and 160 acres west across the road for the same purpose. Some of my happiest and most pleasant recollections are of the years we spent on the Young farm when I was between the ages of three and six.

I had a bobtailed maltese gray cat and a little black-and-tan dog not much bigger than the cat. The old cat was named Bob, because one day when he was asleep in front of the big fireplace in the dining room a coal of fire popped out, lit on the end of his tail, and burned off about an inch of it. I can well remember his yowls, and I can see him yet as he ran up the corner of the room all the way to the ceiling. The little dog was called Tandy because of his black-and-tan color.

These two animals followed Vivian and me everywhere we went, and me alone when Vivian was asleep or too tired to wander over the farm. I was missed on one occasion and was discovered in a cornfield a half mile from the house, enjoying the antics of the cat and dog catching field mice. . . .

My grandfather Young would take me to the Belton Fair, when it was running, in a big two-wheeled cart with high wheels like the one that used to be shown hitched to Nancy Hanks, the great trotter. I would sit in the judges' stand with Grandpa and watch the races, eat striped candy and peanuts, and have the best time a kid ever had.

From *Memoirs by Harry S. Truman; Volume One, Year of Decisions.* Published by Doubleday & Company, Inc., 1955.

had just the happiest childhood that could ever be imagined. My brother, Vivian, and I and two or three of the neighborhood boys used to have a great time playing in the pasture south of the house out at Grandview. There was forty acres in bluegrass, and it had a little draw that ran through it, and there was a spring right in the middle. And we used to catch tadpoles and have a big time over that.

It was a wonderful place for small boys to enjoy themselves. There wasn't any place they could go that they'd get lost, although once in a while one of them would wander over in the cornfield and get lost. I did myself. I had a dog, a little black and tan dog named Tandy, and I also had a big Maltese cat named Bob. . . .

Bob and Tandy always followed me everywhere I went, so when I got lost over in the cornfield, my folks could watch this dog and cat working in and out among the cornstalks, catching field mice. I must have been three and a half or four years old, and I suppose I got a good spanking for running away. I don't remember the spanking, but I do remember the trip through the cornfield.

Those were most pleasant periods of time. We had a great big swing out in the backyard in one of the big old elm trees that was there. It's gone now. And we had a hammock made out of barrel staves that hung on the north porch. And even after we moved to Independence and began to go to school, in the summertime we would go out to Grandview and spend some happy times during the vacation, my brother and I together and sometimes each one of us by himself. . . .

I once read some place that a happy childhood is a very, very rare thing, and I'm sure that that is true, but I can honestly say I had one. . . . Of course, we didn't have all the places to go and things to do that kids do now, and a lot of them don't see how they can get along if they don't have them. But I guess if you don't know what you're missing, you don't miss it, and so, of course, when I was a boy, we didn't have cars and movies and television and radio, none of that. We played. My mother played, and my sister and I played the piano, and we always had a houseful of books, and we read.

And of course, we all had our chores to do, and we went to bed early and got up early and were always busy.

From *Plain Speaking: An Oral Biography of Harry S. Truman* by Merle Miller. Copyright © 1973, 1974 by Merle Miller. Reprinted by permission of The Putnam Publishing Group.

Truman graduated from Independence High School in 1901. He had hoped to go to college, but his father's deepening financial troubles demanded instead that he go to work. Within a year of his high school graduation, Truman began work as a mailroom clerk at the Kansas City Star. Harry was a popular student with classmates and teachers alike. While not the best student in the class, he was enthusiastic and devoted to his studies. He and classmate Charlie Ross once spent an entire month engrossed in the project of building a replica of one of Caesar's bridges across the Rhine which they had read about in Latin class. ABOVE: The Independence High School class of 1901. Harry Truman is fourth from the left in the back row. In the second row, far right, is one of Truman's classmates who would one day figure largely in his life, Bess Wallace, his future wife. Photo courtesy Harry S. Truman Library

Young Harry Truman was devoted to his mother and he almost invariably stayed out of trouble. He was, a boyhood friend recalled, the type of boy other parents used as an example for their own children. ABOVE: Truman as a boy of approximately twelve years. Kept from rough play by his worries over breaking his expensive glasses, Truman filled his childhood hours reading. As an adult, he liked to brag that he had read every book in the Independence Public Library. Photo courtesy Harry S. Truman Library

A FARMER'S LIFE

BY HARRY S. TRUMAN

Truman gave up his dreams of a college education to go to work and help support his family, yet the life he made for himself in Kansas City was colored neither by bitterness nor regret. He was, in fact, thrilled by the bustling atmosphere of the big city. After jobs as a mailroom clerk, a railroad timekeeper, and a bank clerk, Truman landed a job as an assistant bank teller. In 1906, however, John Truman, who had fallen upon hard times and returned to the Grandview farm to make a new start, called Harry home to help. *RIGHT: The Young farmhouse at Grandview. Solomon and Harriet Young, Truman's maternal grandparents, first settled on this land in 1844.* Photo courtesy Modern Woodmen of America Archives

For eleven years, Harry Truman was a farmer. He grew corn and potatoes and experimented with crop rotation. He learned to drive a gangplow, to tend to sick livestock, to mend fences and to fix broken machinery. It was hard, physical work, but it was honest work with true rewards; working side by side with his father, Truman discovered that he loved the challenge of working the land and making things grow. *RIGHT: A herd of sheep graze in front of the Young family farmhouse in Grandview, Missouri. On the porch is Martha Truman, Harry's mother. When Harry left to serve in World War I, she and his younger sister were left with the full responsibility of running the farm.* Photo courtesy Harry S. Truman Library

A farmer's life is not a lonely life at all. You have the best time in the world on a farm like ours. You've always got the stock to take care of, and you've got people coming in to talk to you about whether you can help them out in harvesting the wheat or planting the corn or whatever else is necessary in the neighborhood. I was very active in the farm bureau out there and later in the 4-H and other organizations of that kind.

We had six hundred acres at the time, finest land you'd ever find anywhere. We raised everything—corn, wheat, oats, clover—and we rotated them. I was very much interested in the creation of things that come out of the ground.

I helped my brother and my father to sow oats, plow corn, and sow clover. And in the long run we improved production of the farm nearly fifty percent. . . . I had a gang-plow made by the Henderson Manufacturing Company, and I used that with four horses or two horses and two mules, whatever we had available. That was the way we plowed.

Then the land had to be harrowed, and I enjoyed that. It gave me plenty of time to think. Farmers really all have time to think, and some of them do it, and those are the ones who have made it possible for us to have free government. That's what Jefferson was writing about. Farmers have more time to think than city people do. . . .

The most peaceful thing in the world is riding behind a mule, plowing a field. It's the calmest and most peaceful thing in the world, and while there's some danger that you may, like the fella said, get kicked in the head by a mule and end up believing everything you read in the papers, the chances are you'll do your best thinking that way. And that's why I've always thought and said that farmers are the smartest people in the world.

My father used to trade mules, and he knew a lot about them. He didn't have to look at a mule's teeth to tell how old he was. All he had to do was look at him, and he was never wrong.

A tractor will never be as satisfactory as a mule. It makes a noise, for one thing, and noise interferes with a man's thoughts.

But plowing a field with a mule is the most satisfying thing a man can do. And at the end of the day, looking over what you've done, you can feel a real sense of accomplishment, and that's a very rare thing.

From *Plain Speaking: An Oral Biography of Harry S. Truman* by Merle Miller. Copyright © 1973, 1974 by Merle Miller. Reprinted by permission of The Putnam Publishing Group.

Grandview felt isolated after the years in Independence and Kansas City, but Truman became an active, well-known member of his rural community. He joined the Masons and the Farm Bureau and became a full partner with his father in the Young farm. Whether he imagined that his future lay elsewhere we cannot know. In a letter to his future wife, Bess, written in 1911, Truman praised the American farmer as the solid foundation on which the democracy was laid, but added his belief that "Every farmer thinks he's as good as the President or perhaps a little better." LEFT: Harry, his mother, and grandmother Young outside the farmhouse at Grandview. Harry made a good living off the farm; in a good year his share of profits was as much as $2,000. At nearly six hundred acres, the farm was one of the largest in the area. Photo courtesy Harry S. Truman Library

HARRY AND BESS

BY ROBERT H. FERRELL

All the while he farmed, Harry was courting Bess Wallace, by all accounts the only girl he ever loved. Today, their courtship seems a glimpse of a bygone age, so gentle and restrained was it, compared to "courtships" today; but the tender dignity of their courting and the loving respect of their marriage reflected Harry's character and values perhaps even more than his remarkable public life could. "I guess I am something of a freak . . . ," wrote Harry to Bess, shortly after he was twenty-seven and she had turned down his first proposal of marriage. "I really never had any desire to make love to a girl just for the fun of it, and you have always been the reason. I have never met a girl in my life that you were not the first to be compared with her, to see wherein she was lacking and she always was."

Although Harry's public life featured a long series of capable responses to surprising events, his domestic life took a direction made by choice in his youth and pursued unswervingly ever after. For Harry Truman, Bess was the foundation of a life he had always hoped for and never really expected. His grateful wonder at her affection for him still shines in even the last letters he wrote to her when they had been married many years. In the beginning of their serious courtship, Harry could scarcely believe that Bess would consider him as a suitor. "I have been so afraid you were not even going to let me be your good friend," he told her. "To be even in that class is something." He had no

Bess Wallace was, in the words of Harry Truman, all that a woman could be, "possibly and impossibly." Born Elizabeth Virginia Wallace on February 13, 1885, in Independence, Missouri, Bess was the daughter of David Wallace, a local public official, and Madge Gates Wallace, the daughter of one of Independence's leading citizens. Intelligent, popular, and pretty, Bess earned top grades at school and excelled at athletics. To Truman, son of a country farmer, Bess was at once irresistible and out of reach. ABOVE: Bess Wallace at age four. Photo courtesy Harry S. Truman Library

reason to expect that much would come of the acquaintanceship once their school days were over and he still had made what appeared to be very little impression on Bess. She always had several boy friends, and Harry was not even a member of her social group.

In 1903, however, Bess's carefree life changed abruptly. Mary Paxton, who lived next door, was awakened at five one morning by her father. "Go over to see Bess," he whispered urgently. "Mr. Wallace has killed himself." Mary found her friend walking back and forth behind the Wallace house. Her hands were clenched, her face set; she was not crying. Mary could think of nothing to say, so she paced silently along beside Bess as the gray light turned into morning. . . .

No one inside the Wallace household ever spoke openly of David Wallace again, though somewhat later Mrs. Wallace told Mary Paxton that she felt utterly humiliated by the suicide. . . . she sent Bess to Barstow, a private finishing school in Kansas City. Bess did not board there, but continued to live at home. Mrs. Wallace probably leaned heavily on Bess, who at eighteen was now mature enough to be her mother's confidante. As well as having the sole responsibility for bringing up three sons, Mrs. Wallace had been left with a deep sense of shame. Later on, "Mother Wallace" (as she came to be called) became a force to be reckoned with, not only in her own household, but later in Harry's. He learned to tread lightly with Bess where her mother was concerned, and the frame of his domestic life always had room for his mother-in-law until she died in 1952.

Perhaps her mother's sorrows and her three young brothers' needs kept Bess from making a marriage with one of her other suitors. For whatever reason, she was still single and at home on Delaware Street when Harry found his first real chance to court her seriously. One day in 1910, Harry was visiting Aunt Ella Noland and her daughters Nellie and Ethel, who by then had moved to 216 North Delaware, a little house right across the street from 219. His Aunt Ella mentioned that she had a cake plate of Mrs. Wallace's that needed returning, and (according to Margaret Truman, who heard the story from family talk) Harry seized the plate "with something approaching the speed of light" and took it across the street. When Bess answered his knock, the courtship was on.

June 22, 1911

Dear Bessie:

From all appearances I am not such a very pious person, am I? The elements evidently mistook one of my wishes for dry instead of wet. I guess we'll all have to go to drinking whiskey if it doesn't rain very soon. Water and potatoes will soon be as much of a luxury as pineapples and diamonds.

Speaking of diamonds, would you wear a solitaire on your left hand should I get it? Now that is a rather personal or pointed question provided you take it for all it means. You know, were I an Italian or a poet I would commence and use all the luscious language of two continents. I am not either but only a kind of good-for-nothing American farmer. I've always had a sneakin' notion that some day maybe I'd amount to something. I doubt it now though like everything. It is a family failing of ours to be poor financiers. I am blest that way. Still that doesn't keep me from having always thought you were all that a girl could be possibly and impossibly. You may not have guessed it but I've been crazy about you ever since we went to Sunday school together. But I never had the nerve to think you'd even look at me. I don't think so now but I can't keep from telling you what I think of you. . . .

Say, Bessie, you'll at least let me keep on being good friends won't you? I know I am not good enough to be anything more but you don't know how I'd like to be. Maybe you think I won't wait your answer to this in suspense.

Still if you turn me down, I'll not be thoroughly disappointed for it's no more than I expect. . . .

Please write as soon as you feel that way. The sooner, the better pleased I am.

More than sincerely,

Harry

to Independence much more often. Although she had other boy friends, Harry gradually became her acknowledged suitor. In June 1911, he sent her a letter complaining that if the drought they were having continued, "water and potatoes will soon be as much of a luxury as pineapples and diamonds." "Speaking of diamonds," he went on, "would you wear a solitaire on your left hand should I get it?" For several pages he apologized and stumbled, protesting that if he were "an Italian or a poet" he would use all the luscious language of two continents" to persuade her. He called himself a "kind of good-for-nothing American farmer." "I've always had a sneakin' notion that some day maybe I'd amount to something. I doubt it now though like everything. It is a family failing of ours to be poor financiers. I am blest that way."

He didn't offer much promise beyond devotion and he wasn't surprised when Bess turned him down—only pleased that she didn't ridicule him. He thanked her for listening to his declaration of love. "You see I never have had any desire to say such things to anyone else. All my girl friends think I am a cheerful idiot and a confirmed old bach. They really don't know the reason nor ever will." Finally, in 1917, after seven years and dozens of letters and as many visits as the "good-for-nothing farmer" could manage, Bess accepted Harry's proposal.

At first he and a friend, Stanley Hall, went "sparking" together, driving Stanley's horse and buggy to Stanley's girl's house in Dodson, a small cluster of homes and shops in south Kansas City several miles north of the Grandview farm. Harry would then take a street car into Kansas City and another over to Independence, a ride of almost an hour. Or else he caught the train at Grandview and rode half an hour north to a junction named Sheffield, and then took a street car.

By 1914 these trips became too time-consuming for an increasingly successful farmer, and Harry paid $600 for a 1911 Stafford. . . . Thereafter he was able to travel to see Bess more easily, although the pressures of the farm kept him from getting

From *Truman: A Centenary Remembrance* by Thames and Hudson, Ltd., Robert H. Ferrell. Copyright © 1984 by Thames and Hudson, Ltd. Used by permission of Viking Penguin, a division of Penguin Books USA Inc.

Harry and Bess met in Sunday school as children. Truman claimed to have fallen in love at first sight, but Bess took little notice of young Harry. After their high school graduation, Harry went to Kansas City and later to Grandview, while Bess remained in Independence, where, in 1903, her peaceful world was thrown into turmoil by her father's suicide. Bess, her mother, and her three younger brothers, devastated by this tragedy, took refuge at the Gates family home at 219 North Delaware Street. It was there, in 1910, that Truman renewed his efforts to capture Bess's attention. *RIGHT: Bess in 1901.* Photo courtesy Harry S. Truman Library

Grandview, November 4, 1913

Dear Bess:

Your letter has made a confirmed optimist out of me sure enough. I know now that everything is good and grand and this footstool is a fine place to be. I have been all up in the air, clear above earth ever since it came. I guess you thought I didn't have much sense Sunday, but I just couldn't say anything— only just sit and look. It doesn't seem real that you should care for me. I have always hoped you would but some way feared very much you wouldn't. You know I've always thought that the best man in the world is hardly good enough for any woman. But when it comes to the best girl in all the universe caring for an ordinary gink like me—well, you have to let me get used to it.

Do you want to be a farmer? or shall I do some other business. When Mamma wins her suit and we get all the lawyers and things out of the way I will then have a chance for myself. We intend to raise a four-hundred-acre wheat crop, which if it hits will put us out of the woods. If we lose, which I don't think about, it will mean starting all over for me. You may be sure I'm not going to wait till I'm Montana's chief executive to ask you to be Mrs. Governor, but I sure want to have a decent place to ask you to. I'm hoping it won't be long. I wish it was tomorrow. Let's get engaged anyway to see how it feels. No one need know it but you and me until we get ready to tell it any-way. If you see a man you think more of in the meantime, engagements are easy enough broken. I've always said I'd have you or no one and that's what I mean to do. . . .

Bess, why am I an enigma? I try to be just what I am and tell the truth about as much as the average person. If there's anything you don't under-stand, I'll try and explain or remedy it. I feel very much stuck up at being called one, especially by you, for I always labored under the impression that it took smart people to be one. This letter seems to me to be more erratic and incoherent than the last, but you shouldn't blame me very much because I'm all puffed up and hilarious and happy and anything else that happens to a fellow when he finds his lady love thinks more of him than the rest of the beasts. Send me a letter quick. If I can raise business reasons enough to please Papa, I hope to see you before Sunday.

Most sincerely,

Harry

Years apart did little to quiet Truman's ardor; he arrived on Bess's doorstep one summer night in 1910 as smitten as ever. Bess, devoted to her widowed mother, was hesitant, but Tru-man was equally persistent and a courtship slowly developed. His hours on the farm were long and the trip into Independence a difficult one, so Truman kept in close touch through fre-quent letters. He wrote to Bess of farm life, of his aspirations for the future, and, guardedly at first, of his feelings for her. By the time he left for World War I, Truman had convinced Bess that they belonged together; when he returned from the war they were married. *ABOVE: Harry and Bess Truman pose with their wedding party on the day of their marriage, June 28, 1919.* Photo courtesy Harry S. Truman Library

Diary June 5, 1945

Got back to the White House at 10:30. Called the Madam and talked to her and my baby girl (she doesn't like that designation). I can't help wanting to talk to my sweetheart and my baby every night. I'm a damn fool I guess because I could never get excited or worked up about gals or women. I only had one sweetheart from the time I was six. I saw her in Sunday School at the Presbyterian Church in Independence when my mother took me there at that age and afterwards in the fifth grade at the Ott School in Independence when her Aunt Nannie was our teacher and she sat behind me. She sat behind me in the sixth, seventh, and High School grades and I thought she was the most beautiful and the sweetest person on earth—and I am still of that opinion after twenty-six years of being married to her. I'm old-fashioned, I guess. But it's a happy state to labor under in this terrible job I fell heir to on Apr. 12, '45.

Blair House, Washington, D.C.
June 29, 1949

Dear Bess:

Well, the first day has gone by thirty years ago! I need no commiseration, only congratulations.

Thirty years ago I hoped to make you a happy wife and a happy mother. Did I? I don't know. All I can say [is] I've tried. There is no one in the world anyway who can look down on you or your daughter. That means much to me, but I've never cared for social position or rank for myself except to see that those dear to me were not made to suffer for my shortcomings. . . .

We can never tell what is in store for us. I'm very sure that if you'd been able to see into the future on May 8, 1919, when we had our final argument, you'd have very definitely turned your back on what was coming.

Business failure, with extra responsibility coming, political defeat at the same time. Almost starvation in Washington those first ten years and then hell and repeat from 1944 to date. But I wouldn't change it, and I hope you wouldn't.

Margie is one in ten million, there's none to compare with her mother. I had a good mother and so have you and a good sister. My brother is himself but in the end "right." Yours are the same sort, so—what have we had but the best of luck and a most happy thirty years. Hope we can have thirty more equally as happy without so much responsibility. . . .

Hope you have a good weekend—I'm going to try as best I can to have one—it would be so much better if you were here.

Lots and lots of love to you. . . .

Harry

LEFT: *Harry and Bess on the porch of the house at 219 North Delaware Street in 1953. It was at this Independence home, built by Bess's grandfather, George Porterfield Gates, that the Trumans began their courtship in 1910, in which they embarked upon their married life in 1919, and in which they lived out their retirement after Truman left the White House.* Photo by Bradley Smith

CAPTAIN HARRY

BY ROBERT H. FERRELL

Following the declaration of war, Harry Truman soon volunteered for military service. He had enjoyed his National Guard duty, and it was a period in American history when patriotism was an uncomplicated question. As a former member of Battery B in Kansas City, Harry now helped in the task of bringing in new recruits. The enlarged Batteries B and C (the latter in Independence) were formed into a regiment consisting of six batteries—the 129th Field Artillery. Harry's efforts had brought in so many men, that he told his fellow workers in the armory that he thought he should be a sergeant. Instead, they elected him—as was still the custom in the National Guard—a first lieutenant in Battery F.

Truman's army experience, like that of so many Americans, changed his life, although for some years he did not see where it would take him. . . . In the army, Harry had a chance for the first time to show a gift for leadership and a staunch devotion to his ideal that "One fellow is just as good as another." When Harry went to France in the spring of 1918, he was promoted to captain. In July he was given command of Battery D, the most unruly battery in the regiment. All Irish and German Catholics from Rockhurst

In the spring of 1917, Harry Truman was thirty-three years old. His father had died in 1914, leaving Harry to manage the Grandview farm on his own. He had been out of the National Guard for six years and was two years past the draft's age limit. He had poor eyesight, was the sole supporter of his mother and sister, and was engaged to be married. He was, in short, neither required nor expected to serve in World War I. But Harry Truman was, in his own words, "stirred heart and soul" by President Wilson's call to help "make the world safe for democracy." It was idealism, combined with a romantic vision of the noble cause, that drove Truman to volunteer to serve in World War I. Like countless other American young men, Truman wanted to be a part of history. In May of 1917 Truman rejoined the National Guard; a short time later his unit was made part of the 129th Field Artillery of the U.S. Army. LEFT: The identification card carried by Captain Truman during World War I. Photo courtesy Harry S. Truman Library

College, a Jesuit high school in Kansas City, the two-hundred boys of Battery D were a rollicking, hot-tempered band who had broken three previous commanders.

The night Harry took over the battery he announced that he was in charge, and turned the group over to the first sergeant for the order to the men to fall out. According to one of the battery's members, the trouble started at once: "And then we gave Captain Truman the Bronx cheer, that's a fact." At the time, the captain chose to ignore their disrespectful gesture, but next morning, on the bulletin board, half the noncommissioned officers and most of the first-class privates were "busted." "And then" remembered Vere C. (Pup) Leigh, a member of the battery, "we knew that we had a different 'cat' to do business with than we had up to that time. He didn't hesitate at all."

The men of Battery D came to idolize their commander because he was tough and fair—and courageous. He once got them out of a tight fix, the so-called "Battle of Who Run," when after the Americans fired five hundred rounds of gas shells at the Germans, the enemy returned fire and zeroed their guns in on Truman's battery. The first sergeant panicked and shouted, "Run, boys, they got a bracket on us!" Instantly, the captain was on the scene, eyes flashing, arms flailing, holding the battery in line, shouting at them, calling them all the names he could think of. It was more epithets than most had ever heard. "It took the skin off the ears of those boys. It turned those boys right around," remembered Father L. Curtis Tiernan, regimental chaplain, who was there. Despite the clump and boom of shells, the smoke, the deadly shrapnel flying, the ground heaving, the soldiers stayed. They hitched horses to the caissons and pulled the guns away to safety.

On another occasion, Captain Truman did not hesitate to stand up for one of his men. During a march through Alsace when horses were scarce, a member of Truman's battery suffered a painful ankle injury. Truman put the man up on a horse. When a colonel saw this and demanded that the horse be unburdened, Truman retorted, "You can take these bars off my shoulders, but as long as I'm in charge of this battery the man's going to stay on that horse." The colonel rode away in a huff, and the injured soldier rode on behind his captain. . . .

After the war, the battery's men held reunions year after year on Armistice Day. In 1949, when President Truman invited the "boys" of Battery D to Washington for his inauguration, they marched in single file on each side of the presidential limousine. By then a paunchy, aging group, jauntily swinging canes, they were immensely proud of their moment in the public eye and of their former comrade in arms, their Captain Harry. When they had met that day before breakfast and someone had addressed Harry Truman as "Mr. President," his rejoinder was immediate. "We'll have none of that here," he said. "I'm Captain Harry."

From *Truman: A Centenary Remembrance* by Thames and Hudson, Ltd., Robert H. Ferrell. Copyright © 1984 by Thames and Hudson, Ltd. Used by permission of Viking Penguin, a division of Penguin Books USA Inc.

After training at Camp Doniphan, Oklahoma, Truman went to France, where he attended an elite artillery school for officers. In April of 1918, Captain Harry S. Truman took command of Battery D, a unit with a reputation for unusual rowdiness, and led them into battle.

In almost three months of near-continuous combat, the men of Battery D fought bravely at Saint-Mihiel, on the Meuse-Argonne front, at Verdun, and at Metz. Truman proved himself an able leader. He learned to respect and get along with men from all walks of American life, and he found that through fair and compassionate leadership he could inspire the respect and admiration of those who served under him. The men from Battery D would remain Harry Truman's closest friends for the rest of his life. LEFT: The officers of the 129th Field Artillery at Chateau le Chenay in France. Captain Harry S. Truman is fourth from the left in the second row from the bottom. Photo by U.S. Army Signal Corps, courtesy Harry S. Truman Library

LETTERS FROM A SOLDIER

BY HARRY S. TRUMAN

I have just finished the Regimental Banquet. It was a very solemn affair. Colonel Klemm made us a speech on our duties to God and country, and Lieutenant Colonel Elliott made one on the duties of an artillery officer. They were both from the shoulder and gave us something to think about. I had thought somewhat on both subjects, but not as far as these gentlemen went. According to them, we have placed ourselves in a position of placing the American Government above everything, even our lives. We are expected to do absolutely as we are told. Evidently, if we are ordered to go to Berlin, go we must—or be buried on the way.

I hope Russia saves us the trip, although I'd like to be present when Berlin falls. I tried to call you up this evening hoping that perhaps I'd get asked over to dinner tomorrow but I had only one chance at the phone and it failed. Maybe I can have better luck in the morning. I thought about you all evening, as I hope this letter proves. It was absolutely necessary for me to be present, as the colonel gave us our commissions from the governor. . . . I have felt like a dog all week. It seems that I have caused you to be unhappy by my overenthusiastic action in getting myself sent to war. Two big tears came in Mamma's eyes last night when I started off to Lodge in my soldier clothes. You are the two people in the world that I would rather see smile and that I like to cause to smile, and here I've gone done the opposite to both of you. Perhaps I can make you all happier for it. I'll try my best. Some way I seem to have an ability for getting myself into things by overzealous conduct or anxiety to see them a

> WE HAVE PLACED OURSELVES IN A POSITION OF PLACING THE AMERICAN GOVERNMENT ABOVE EVERYTHING, EVEN OUR LIVES.

success and do not seem to see the consequences to myself or others until the conclusion comes. . . .

Bess, I'm dead crazy to ask you to marry me before I leave but I'm not going to because I don't think it would be right for me to ask you to tie yourself to a prospective cripple—or a sentiment. You, I know, would love me just as much, perhaps more, with one hand as with two, but I don't think I should cause you to do it. Besides, if the war ends happily and I can steal the Russian or German crown jewels, just think what a grand military wedding you can have, get a major general maybe.

If you don't marry me before I go, you may be sure that I'll be just as loyal to you as if you were my wife. I'll not try to exact any promises from you either if you want to go with any other guy, why all right, but I'll be as jealous as the mischief although not begrudging you the good time.

Bess, this is a crazy letter but I'm crazy about you and I can't say all these nutty things to you without making you weep. When you weep, I want to. If you'd looked right closely the other night, you might have discovered it, and a weeping man is an abomination unto the Lord. All I ask is love me always and if I have to be shot I'll try and not have it in the back or before a stone wall, because I'm afraid not to do you honor.

From a letter Truman wrote to Bess from the Densmore Hotel in Kansas City, Missouri, on July 14, 1917.

This is the first opportunity I have had to write you since the day I wrote from the woods before the big drive began. I am very sorry to have been so long but things have happened to me so rapidly I couldn't write. There was no chance to mail them if I could have. The great drive has taken place and I had a part in it, a very small one but nevertheless a part. The experience has been one that I can never forget, one that I don't want to go through again unless the Lord wills but one I'd never have missed for anything. The papers are in the street now saying that the Central Powers have asked for peace, and I was in the drive that did it! I shot out a German battery, shot up his big observation post, and ruined another Battery when it was moving down the road. My excellent Second Lieutenant Zemer and myself were in the front of the infantry lines while I was doing it, and I saw tanks take towns and everything else that there is to see. I brought my Battery forward under fire and never lost a horse nor a man. Had shells fall on all sides and I am as sure as I am sitting here that the Lord was and is with me. I'm not yet dizzy although one or two men in the regiment are.

We are in billets now resting up and I suppose we'll go back in when they need us. I am as fat, healthy, and look as well as I ever did, so don't worry about me because there is no German shell with my name on it. I am glad Fred is going to the university as I believe it is a necessity to a man these days. I've had a university education and then some in the last year. Being a Battery commander is an education in itself. I don't know if I have made a successful one or not, but we've been in and out a couple of times together and I still have the Battery. There were a couple of men hurt this last time but they were not with me, they were on special detail with the ammunition train.

If this peace talk is true and we do get to come home soon, I can tell you a lot of things I can't write about. You will probably hear more than you wish. . . .

Would you meet me in New York and go to the Little Church Around the Corner if I get sent home? We can then go east or west or any old direction you wish for a tour. I have an idea if peace comes that it will be six months before we can get home. I got three letters from you today and I surely did appreciate them. I got three also while I was right up under the German guns and I tell you it sure bolstered up my nerve. We were on the most famous battlefield of the war, in front of the town the Germans couldn't take, and were against the Kaiser's pick but they ran just the same. I hope the censor don't see that.

From a letter Truman wrote to Bess from an unknown location in France, October 6, 1918.

Truman's service in World War I was one of the defining experiences of his life. The friendships that he made during his years in the service lasted a lifetime and gave him a loyal network of supporters across the nation. LEFT: the president marches with former members of Battery D in Little Rock, Arkansas, in June of 1949. Photo by U.S. Army Signal Corps, courtesy National Archives

LEFT: Harry Truman, age four, and his brother, John Vivian Truman, known as Vivian, age two. Harry and Vivian spent idyllic early childhood years exploring the more than six hundred acres of their grandfather Young's farm. While his elder brother went on to a life in politics, Vivian followed the family tradition and made his living as a farmer. Photo by The Kansas City Star

ABOVE: Bess Wallace as a young girl. Bess was an intelligent, self-confident young girl. She excelled at tennis, ice skating, and riding and also played third base on her brothers' baseball team. Photo courtesy Harry S. Truman Library

In the eyes of Independence society, Harry Truman, the son of a country farmer, was no match for Bess Wallace, daughter of one of Independence's leading families. But Truman rose above such class prejudice and proved himself a devoted and worthy suitor. ABOVE: Harry and Bess with friends at the waterworks near Sugar Creek, Missouri, in October 1913. RIGHT: The couple enjoy a fishing trip on the Little Blue River in August 1913. Photos courtesy Harry S. Truman Library

Without his eyeglasses, Truman could barely recognize people standing only a few feet in front of him; to be on the safe side, he brought six pairs of glasses with him to Europe when he served during World War I. RIGHT: Truman in uniform in 1917 at the age of thirty-four. Photo courtesy Harry S. Truman Library

Truman was an original member of his Missouri National Guard unit, but by the time World War I began, he had left the Guard to concentrate on farming. Inspired by patriotism, however, he rejoined the National Guard in 1917 to fight in World War I. ABOVE: Harry S. Truman in his National Guard uniform in 1905 or 1906. Photo courtesy Harry S. Truman Library

After the war, Truman auctioned the equipment from the Young farm to raise the money to open a men's clothing store with his Army buddy Eddie Jacobson. Truman and Jacobson opened its doors in 1919. The store sold shirts, socks, ties, belts, and hats—a good deal of them to Truman's large circle of World War I friends. The store flourished in its first year, but closed in 1922 during a serious recession. Deeply in debt, Truman resisted declaring personal bankruptcy; he made regular payments on his shirt store debts for more than twenty years. ABOVE AND LEFT: Truman and Jacobson, the Kansas City men's clothing store. Photos courtesy Harry S. Truman Library

THE BIRTH OF A POLITICIAN

BY ROBERT H. FERRELL

As a boy, Truman accompanied his father to Democratic party rallies and followed both his parents' lead in supporting Democratic candidates in local and national elections. In 1900, he served as a page at the Democratic National Convention. When he was ten, his mother gave him a four-volume set of books entitled Great Men and Famous Women, volumes which taught him how leaders of principle and courage can shape history and which inspired him to imagine for himself a career in politics. Still, in his own words, his entry into public service "just happened." ABOVE: Judge Harry S. Truman votes in Independence, Missouri, in 1934. Photo by Roger Reynolds, The Kansas City Star

One afternoon in 1921, a young friend from Harry Truman's army days stopped into the clothing store. He was Jim Pendergast, a lieutenant in the 129th Field Artillery and nephew of Tom Pendergast, head of the Democratic Party machine in Kansas City. With him was his father, Mike Pendergast, a leading local politician. "Run for office," they said to Truman.

The office they had in mind was that of judge (or commissioner) of the rural eastern district of Jackson County, of which Mike Pendergast was Democratic Party "Boss." Truman was interested; he had been working regularly with Mike Pendergast's Tenth Ward political club since before 1914. The members of the Tenth Ward democratic Club were, like all Pendergast Democrats, known as Goats, while the forces of another prominent Kansas City Democrat, Joseph B. Shannon, were called Rabbits. When Truman became road overseer in 1914, his duties included attending the Goats' weekly Thursday-night meetings.

The Pendergasts' first proposal that Truman should run for office came at a time when the haberdashery was still doing well, and he refused to leave the business, but when they came back with the same proposal a year later, he eagerly accepted. His movement toward politics had been more a matter of drift than drive, through chance associations and one thing leading to another. During the war, Truman had sometimes been heard to say that he might run for Congress, and that if he were elected he would give a comeuppance to the Regular Army officers who bedeviled him and his men. Jim Pendergast had heard this talk, and he knew that his political family—firmly entrenched in the city, heavily dependent upon their Roman Catholic ties—could use a good

Baptist such as Harry Truman who had roots in farming areas. In 1922, the party machine needed someone for election to the three man county court to help defeat the presiding judge. . . . Truman was their candidate.

He came from a family of dedicated Democrats. One of his friends during the presidential years, George Allen, once remarked to Truman's mother that, where he came from in Mississippi, he never saw a Republican until he was twelve. "George," replied Mrs. Truman, "you didn't miss much." There weren't many Republicans to be seen in Missouri either. In Kansas City, they were hardly recognized, so strong was the Democratic Party's hold. Tom Evans, a later friend of Truman's and owner of Crown Drugstores and radio station KCMO, used to say that in his part of the city he had never seen a Republican. The real fights for election were in the Democratic primaries; November merely confirmed the primary decisions.

> *HE CAME FROM A FAMILY OF DEDICATED DEMOCRATS. ONE OF HIS FRIENDS DURING THE PRESIDENTIAL YEARS, GEORGE ALLEN, ONCE REMARKED TO TRUMAN'S MOTHER THAT, WHERE HE CAME FROM IN MISSISSIPPI, HE NEVER SAW A REPUBLICAN UNTIL HE WAS TWELVE. "GEORGE," REPLIED MRS. TRUMAN, "YOU DIDN'T MISS MUCH."*

Truman always believed that anyone who wished to be a politician had to learn the art, which to him meant assessing opponents, anticipating issues, then meeting the people: ringing doorbells, speaking in church basements, going to one meeting after another. It was old-fashioned stumping, the way the party of the people, the Democratic Party, had traditionally advanced itself. Truman did what was required of him during the campaign of 1922, but his speeches were not memorable. Indeed, the first was a near disaster. "I recall it very vividly," he wrote many years later. "It wasn't a speech, it was a thoroughly rattled fellow on the platform who couldn't say a word. . . . They had a meeting down at Lee's Summit. They had all the candidates there and when it came my turn to talk, I couldn't talk. I was scared to death!" Then and for many years afterward, Truman was an ineffective public speaker. His flat voice—when he found it—simply put audiences to sleep.

Fortunately for Truman in 1922, his army friends laced his audiences and made up in enthusiastic support what the candidate himself lacked in oratory. They loudly applauded Captain Harry. . . . Family, church, and Masonic connections also helped, but the army was crucial. Truman knew this and much later commented, "My whole political career is based upon my war service and war associates." His own Battery D and the 129th Field Artillery as a whole were the foundations of victory in the 1922 election.

Much has been made by Truman's biographers of his remarkable work during his ten years of service on the county court—he was eastern judge from 1923 to 1925 and then, after a defeat because of a falling-out of the Pendergast and Shannon factions, ran for presiding judge, won, and served two four-year terms between 1927 and 1935. Truman proved a model administrator in Jackson County, which then comprised a half million people. He foresaw the need for road building, because of increasing numbers of automobiles and trucks, and insisted on good concrete roads. . . . He inherited a public system of nearly 1,100 miles of roads—70 unimproved, 670 graded and oiled, and 350 paved. Built by county judges who knew little about engineering, the existing roads cost $900,000 a year to maintain, and repairs consisted only of a little surface work on the worn places.

Something had to be done. Truman appointed a nonpartisan board of two engineers, one of them a Republican, who proposed to build an entirely new system, consisting of 224 miles of properly constructed highway. As presiding judge, he then arranged two large bond issues, $6.5 million in 1928 and $7.9 million in 1931, mostly for roads. He tried to distribute the new network so that no farm in the county was more than two-and-a-half miles from a concrete road. Then, in 1932, Truman arranged for the publication of a 122-page illustrated booklet—*Jackson County: Results of County Planning*—showing the progress made in road building and also the proposed remodeling of the courthouse in Independence and the new skyscraper courthouse in Kansas City erected during his administration.

From: *Truman: A Centenary Remembrance* by Thames and Hudson, Ltd., Robert H. Ferrell. Copyright © 1984 by Thames and Hudson, Ltd. Used by permission of Viking Penguin, a division of Penguin Books USA Inc.

> *I consider political experience absolutely necessary, because a man who understands politics understands free government. Our government is by the consent of the people, and you have to convince a majority of the people that what you are trying to do is right and in their interest. If you are not a politician, you cannot do it.*
>
> —HARRY S. TRUMAN

In 1922, the haberdashery that Truman had opened after the war with old Army buddy Eddie Jacobson fell victim to recession. The two men were suddenly and deeply in debt. Harry Truman, close to forty years old and with a wife to support, needed a job. When another friend from his World War I days, Jim Pendergast, suggested that Truman run for eastern judge of Jackson County—with the full support of the powerful Pendergast political machine—Truman agreed. Thus humbly began Harry Truman's road to the White House. *ABOVE:* Senator-elect Harry S. Truman, presiding judge of Jackson County, at his desk in the Independence Courthouse in 1934. Truman's years as county judge were both enlightening and disillusioning for him. As he discovered his own love of public service, he discovered also the dishonesty and corruption that was rampant in local politics. Truman once wrote to Bess that, had he chosen the path of corruption, he could have made more than a million and a half dollars while serving as judge. Photo by The Kansas City Star. Campaigning in the small towns and farm communities of Missouri in 1922, Truman proved a less than inspirational public speaker, but a natural at mixing with the electorate. With the help of the Pendergasts and with many long days on the road, Truman won election as eastern judge, an administrative post with responsibility for county money, employees, and road contracts. Despite a good record on the job, Truman lost his bid for reelection; but in two years in office he had gained something invaluable—a true sense of purpose and direction. In 1926, confident that his future lay in public service, Truman again entered the political fray, this time as a successful candidate for presiding judge, a senior position to his previous post. *LEFT:* Harry S. Truman is sworn in as judge of the county court of Jackson County, Missouri, in January of 1931. Truman was above reproach in his years as judge. In one election, the worst scandal the opposition could come up with was that he had once voted for a Republican. When Truman explained that this Republican was an old Army friend, this minor misstep was forgiven. Photo courtesy Harry S. Truman Library

Tomorrow I'll be forty-nine and for all the good I've done the forty might as well be left off. Take it all together though the experience has been worthwhile; I'd like to do it again. I've been in a railroad, bank, farm, war, politics, love (only once and it still sticks), been busted and still am and yet I have stayed an idealist. I still believe that my sweetheart is the ideal woman and that my daughter is her duplicate. I think that for all the horrors of war it still makes a man if he's one to start with. Politics should make a thief, a roué, and a pessimist of anyone, but I don't believe I'm any of them and if I can get the Kansas City courthouse done without scandal no other judge will have done as much, and then maybe I can retire as collector and you and the young lady can take some European and South American tours when they'll do you most good; or maybe go to live in Washington and see all the greats and near greats in action. We'll see.

In two four-year terms, Judge Truman cut county debt, boosted county credit rating, and improved local roads. Around Jackson County and all of Missouri, Judge Truman earned a reputation for honesty, integrity, hard work, and productivity. LEFT: Using a multiple signature machine, Judge Truman signs checks in his office in 1927. Photo by Kansas City *Journal Post*, courtesy Harry S. Truman Library

I was beginning to realize—forty years before I had any thought of becoming President of the United States—that almost all current events in the affairs of governments and nations have their parallels and precedents in the past. It was obvious to me even then that a clear understanding of administrative problems presupposes a knowledge of similar ones as recorded in history and of their disposition. Long before I ever considered going into public life I had arrived at the conclusion that no decisions affecting the people should be made impulsively, but on the basis of historical background and careful consideration of the facts as they exist at the time.

History taught me that the leader of any country, in order to assume his responsibilities as a leader, must know the history of not only his own country but of all the other great countries, and that he must make the effort to apply this knowledge to the decisions that have to be made for the welfare of all the people.

—HARRY S. TRUMAN, From *Memoirs by Harry S. Truman: Volume One, Year of Decisions.*
Published by Doubleday & Company, Inc., 1955

THE SENATOR FROM MISSOURI

BY HARRY S. TRUMAN

It was a great day for me on January 3, 1935, when I entered the chamber of the United States Senate to take my seat for the first time. I had always thought of the Senate as one of the world's great deliberative bodies, and I was aware of the honor and responsibility that had been given to me by the people of my state.

Although I was nearly fifty-one years old at the time, I was as timid as a country boy arriving on the campus of a great university for his first year. There was much to learn about the traditions of the Senate, and I can honestly say that I went there to learn all I could about my new role in the federal government. I realized that the more I knew about it the better I could perform my duties as a senator. Even before I had left Kansas City for Washington I had read the biographies of every member of the Senate and had studied every piece of information I could find on our chief lawmaking body. I was to learn later that the estimates of the various members which I formed in advance were not always accurate. I soon found that, among my ninety-five colleagues, the real business of the Senate was carried on by unassuming and conscientious men, not by those who managed to get the most publicity.

I very distinctly remember taking the oath as a senator. As an officer in the Army and as a county official, I had probably taken the same oath a dozen times, but now it seemed far more impressive than at any other time until I took the oath of office as President in 1945. My colleague, Senator Bennett Clark, escorted me to the Vice-President and in turn escorted me back to my seat.

As I walked back to my seat from the desk of the Vice-President I had a prayer in my heart for wisdom to serve the people acceptably. And it was not only the people of Missouri I had in mind, but the people of every part of the United States, for I felt myself to be a representative of all Americans.

The first meeting of the Senate, which had convened at noon, was over in a very short time. At two o'clock it was called back into session for an announcement. The House of Representatives, we were told, had a quorum present, had elected its officers, and was prepared to meet jointly with the Senate on the following day to hear the annual message to the Congress by the president of the United States. With that announcement made, the Senate adjourned. My first day as senator was officially over, and I looked forward with eager anticipation to the next.

It was after the Senate had adjourned the following day that I began to have the conviction that I was now where I really belonged. I had been pleased by President Roosevelt's address calling for basic reforms to replace the emergency relief measures of his administration. I knew that the program he was enunciating for the welfare and security of all classes of Americans was a program that I could support wholeheartedly. In fact, it was one which I had already put into effect on a local level.

From the long list of bills and resolutions introduced in the Senate during the afternoon session which followed the joint meeting with the House I could see that I was going to be busier than I had ever been in Jackson County if I expected to keep up with all that was going on. The desk in my office . . . was already piled high with documents and correspondence calling for my attention. That night I returned to my new residence at Tilden Gardens . . . with an armload of papers to read and study. I did not realize it then, but that was a practice I was going to keep up for the next eighteen years. . . .

My ten years in the Senate had now begun—years which were to be filled with hard work but which were also to be the happiest ten years of my life.

From *Memoirs by Harry S. Truman; Volume One, Year of Decisions.* Published by Doubleday & Company, Inc., 1955.

*Tomorrow, today, rather, it is 4 A.M., I have to make the most momentous announce-
ment of my life. I have come to the place where all men strive to be at my age, and I
thought two weeks ago that retirement on a virtual pension in some minor county
office was all that was in store for me. When I was a very young boy, my mother gave
me four large books called "Heroes of History." The volumes were classified as "Soldiers and Sailors," "Statesmen and Sages," and two others which I forget now. I spent
most of my time reading those books, "Abbott's Lives," and my mother's big Bible. . . .
They impressed me immensely. I also spent a lot of time on the twentieth chapter of
Exodus and the 5th, 6th, and Seventh chapters of Matthew's gospel. I am still at fifty of
the opinion that there are no other laws to live by. . . .*

*And now I am a candidate for the U.S. Senate. If the Almighty God decides that I
go there, I am going to pray as King Solomon did, for wisdom to do the job.*

—HARRY S. TRUMAN, WRITTEN ON THE EVE OF HIS SENATE CANDIDACY ANNOUNCEMENT, MAY 13–14, 1934

Truman won election to the U.S. Senate in November 1934.
Elected in large part due to the support of the Pendergast
machine—a political machine embroiled in scandal and con-
troversy—Truman, fifty years old and little known outside
Missouri, arrived in Washington with a great deal to prove.
But the new senator worked long hours and kept his mouth
shut and his eyes and ears open. In time, he began to earn in
the Senate the same reputation for hard work, honesty, and
integrity that he had at home in
Missouri. LEFT: Senator Truman
poses in front of a photo of Tom
Pendergast. When scandal
began to swirl around Pendergast, Truman remained faithful.
"I won't," he said, "desert a
sinking ship." Photo by
AP/Wide World Photo. RIGHT:
Senator Truman at the Democratic National Convention in
1936. Photo by Roger
Reynolds, The Kansas City Star

*Merely talking about the
Four Freedoms is not
enough. This is the time for action. No one can any longer doubt the
horrible intentions of the Nazi beasts. We know that they plan the
systematic slaughter throughout all of Europe, not only of the Jews
but of vast numbers of other innocent peoples. . . . Their present
oppressors must know that they will be held directly accountable for
their bloody deeds. To do all this, we must draw deeply on our traditions of aid to the oppressed, and on our great national generosity.
This is not a Jewish problem, it is an American problem—and we
must and we will face it squarely and honorably.*

—SENATOR HARRY S. TRUMAN, APRIL 14, 1943

THE TRUMANS IN WASHINGTON

BY ROBERT H. FERRELL

During these years Truman lived with Bess, their daughter Margaret, who had been born in 1924, and Mother Wallace in a succession of cramped, two-bedroom apartments in Washington. He loved having his family with him—his Bess, whom he still thought of as the light in every day, and his beloved Margie, "my beautiful baby," as he continued to call her even when he was President and she a young woman. Even the indomitable Mother Wallace helped turn the Washington flats into something more like the Independence home he missed. Of course, Bess, her mother, and her daughter missed Independence too, and they often went back. During the whole of the Trumans' time in Washington, Bess never found a laundry that suited her, and the family laundry was sent home to Kansas City to an old local firm. Other things in Washington didn't suit the Trumans very well either. Their life style and values were essentially small-town mid-American, and the family didn't mesh well with Washington high society. Moreover, they had little money for keeping up the image or the pace of Washington life, for they were still paying out campaign debts. Not until 1946 were they finally clear of the burden and able to buy back the family farm, lost to foreclosure by county officials in 1940, at which time Truman's mother and sister were forced to move into a tiny rented house in Grandview.

The Washington apartments varied, year after year, as the Trumans frequently rented one only while the Senate was in session. In between times, when office routine or special sessions made Truman's presence in Washington necessary, he lived in hotels near Capitol Hill. . . . Meals he managed when he was alone by taking breakfast in the apartment, lunches at the Senate office building, dinners at the Hot Shoppe of Harvey's. It was neither a glamorous life nor an adventurous one. Mostly it was busy—and when

Margaret, Bess, and Mrs. Wallace went home to Independence, it was lonely. Still, the Truman family looked back on the Senate years as good years—particularly in comparison to the years of strain that came later.

From: *Truman: A Centenary Remembrance* by Thames and Hudson, Ltd., Robert H. Ferrell. Copyright © 1984 by Thames and Hudson, Ltd. Used by permission of Viking Penguin, a division of Penguin Books USA Inc.

Of daughter Margaret, Harry once wrote, "I want her to do everything and have everything and still learn that most people have to work to live, and I don't want her to be a high hat." As parents, the Trumans were never extravagant, but always attentive and loving. In the Gates house, where Margaret spent most of her childhood, she learned the grace and manners of her Grandmother Wallace. On the farm at Grandview, she heard stories of pioneer life and delighted in Mamma Truman's wit and spirit. Margaret became her father's pride and joy, "one in ten million" as Harry wrote to Bess. ABOVE: Senator Truman, Bess, and Margaret at home in Washington in 1942. Photo by Office of War Information, courtesy Harry S. Truman Library

Your card was a lifesaver this morning. I have never in my life spent such a lonesome night. I went "home" at nine-thirty after I'd talked to you and when I opened the apartment door I thought I heard Margaret say, "Hello Dad"—and I asked, well where is mother, as usual, and then I walked all around to make sure I wasn't dreaming, read the Congressional Record, *put a sheet on your bed, and turned in. Every time I'd hear that young lady in the next apartment I would be sure my family were coming in.*

—SENATOR HARRY S. TRUMAN, FROM A 1935 LETTER HOME TO BESS IN INDEPENDENCE

Harry, Bess, and Margaret lived their lives quietly and frugally in Washington. They rented a modest apartment, they rode the trolleys, and they lived on Bess's carefully figured budget. Mrs. Truman learned to enjoy life in Washington; but she always longed for a permanent return to Missouri, and she and Margaret made frequent extended visits to Independence. ABOVE: One of a series of photos depicting a typical day in the life of Senator Truman, part of a rush of publicity after his work on the Senate committee investigating the defense effort. RIGHT: Harry and Bess shop for groceries in Washington. The Trumans were shocked by the cost of living in Washington and found it difficult to make the $10,000 salary Harry received cover even their modest expenses.
Photos by UPI/Corbis-Bettman

THE TRUMAN COMMITTEE

BY HARRY S. TRUMAN

When I was sworn in for the second time as senator on January 3, 1941, this country was preparing for war. We had suddenly realized that we were unprepared to face the dangers that confronted us and had begun a frantic attempt to remedy that situation. We had decided to build a two-ocean navy and to train and arm a million men a year for a period of five years. We had begun to spend money by the billion to accomplish those two purposes. . . .

Our national defense machinery, which had never been quite adequate, suddenly had to be expanded to enormous proportions. Contracts for construction, for supplies, and for munitions were negotiated in desperate haste. Washington was full of people seeking contracts, most of them sincerely desiring to be of help to the government, some seeking only their own selfish interests.

It had become necessary to let enormous contracts for the expansion of airplane plants and for the construction of new ones. Munitions plants were being constructed throughout the nation. Clothing, supplies, munitions, battleships, airplanes, and everything necessary for the defense program were being purchased at a rate never before dreamed of. Some sixteen and a half billions in appropriations were authorized and appropriated for defense. This did not include the appropriation of seven billions for aid to Britain or the four billions for the Army, both of which were pending at the time in the House of Representatives. When these appropriations were completed and authorized, defense expenditures during the first few months of 1941 would exceed twenty-five billions of dollars.

I was concerned about charges that the huge contracts and the immense purchases that resulted from these appropriations were being handled through favoritism. There were rumors that some of the plants had been located on a basis of friendship. I feared that many of the safeguards usually observed in government transactions were being thrown aside and overlooked, although these safeguards would in no way have slowed up the program. I knew, too, that certain lobbyists were seeking the inside track on purchases, contracts, and plant locations. There were rumors of enormous fees being paid to these gentlemen and of purchases having been concentrated among a few manufacturers of supplies.

I saw cliques in labor and in capital, each greedy for gain, while small production plants by the hundreds were being pushed aside and kept inactive by big business. The big fellows, in the name of the government, were putting thousands of small concerns out of business that should have been producing for the total war effort.

I was concerned about these small shops and factories and I tried to figure out how they could be used more effectively in the nation's over-all defense program. Because of the shortage of machine tools, big companies were sometimes attempting to buy, and even to requisition, machines belonging to small businesses. When these machines were moved, workmen had to follow, which added to the concentration of population and created more housing problems. On the other hand, the problem of vacant housing developed in the communities they had left.

I gave a lot of thought to this situation, and when I realized that it was growing increasingly worse, I decided to take a closer look at it. I got into my automobile and started out from Washington to make a little investigation on my own. I drove thirty thousand miles in a great circle through Maryland and from there down to Florida, across to Texas, north through Oklahoma to Nebraska, and back through Wisconsin and Michigan. I visited war camps, defense plants, and other establishments and projects which had some connection with the total war effort of the country, and did not let any of them know who I was.

The trip was an eye-opener, and I came back to Washington convinced that something needed to be done fast. I had seen at first hand that grounds existed for a good many of the rumors that were prevalent in Washington concerning the letting of contracts and the concentration of defense industries in big cities.

I had decided to make a speech on the subject before the Senate in order to emphasize the need for action and call on the Senate for a committee to investigate the situation. Such a committee would have the power of the United States Senate to bring action where it was needed.

From *Memoirs by Harry S. Truman; Volume One, Year of Decisions.* Published by Doubleday & Company, Inc., 1955.

In 1941, Senator Truman launched an independent investigation into American defense plants and Army installations. What he discovered was that in the rush to meet FDR's huge demands for war production, the camps and factories were placing speed and quantity above quality. Truman returned to Washington to ask his fellow senators to form a special committee to conduct a full-scale investigation. The Senate Special Committee to Investigate the National Defense Program began work in April of 1941. LEFT: Senator Truman conducts an inspection of Camp Crowder, Missouri, in August of 1944. Photo by U.S. Army, courtesy Harry S. Truman Library

The Truman Committee began with seven members, all but one junior senators. As they proved their worth, however, membership and funding were increased. Their motto: "There is no substitute for a fact." ABOVE: The Committee inspects at Camp Crowder. Photo by U.S. Army, courtesy Harry S. Truman Library

The Truman Committee's aim was neither to indict any individual nor to subvert the defense efforts of the Roosevelt administration, but rather to improve the country's war production. Between 1941 and 1944, the committee exposed nearly $15 billion in waste. Truman won almost universal praise for his work. In March 1943 Time magazine called him "scrupulously honest"; Look magazine named the senator one of ten Americans making a valuable contribution to the war effort. ABOVE: Truman and Floyd Odlum study routes followed by defense trains. Photo by AP/Wide World Photos. LEFT: Charles P. Clark, associate chief counsel; Truman; Senator Owen Brewster; and Senator Joseph H. Ball of the Truman Committee conduct hearings in Washington, D.C. Photo courtesy Harry S. Truman Library

TRUMAN AND FDR

BY HARRY S. TRUMAN

Early in 1944 some of my friends began to suggest to me that I become a candidate for Vice-President. I had never entertained such an idea, and whenever the suggestion was made I brushed it aside. I was doing the job I wanted to do; it was one that I liked, and I had no desire to interrupt my career in the Senate. . . .

In July 1944, as I was about to leave my home in Independence for the opening of the convention in Chicago the telephone rang. It was Jimmy Byrnes calling from Washington. He told me that President Roosevelt had decided on him as the new nominee for Vice-President, and he asked me if I would nominate him at the convention. I told him that I would be glad to do it if the President wanted him. . . .

Before I left for Chicago there was another call. It was Alben Barkley, the majority leader of the Senate, asking if I would nominate him for Vice-President at the convention. I told him that Byrnes had just called me with the same request and that I had already promised to place his name before the convention.

When I arrived in Chicago I had breakfast with Sidney Hillman, who was a power in the labor faction of the convention. I asked him if he would support Byrnes. He said he would not, that there were only two men besides Henry Wallace he would support. They were William O. Douglas, justice of the Supreme Court, and Harry S. Truman. . . . I told him that I was not a candidate. . . .

On Tuesday evening of convention week, National Chairman Bob Hannegan came to see me and told me unequivocally that President Roosevelt wanted me to run with him on the ticket. This astonished me greatly, but I was still not convinced. Even when Hannegan showed me a longhand note written on a scratch pad from the President's desk which said, "Bob, it's Truman. F.D.R.," I still could not be sure that this was Roosevelt's intent, although I later learned that the handwriting in the note was the President's own.

One thing that contributed to my confusion was my knowledge of a letter which the President had written earlier in which he stated that he would be satisfied with either Wallace or Douglas. He had also made a public statement to the effect that, if he were a delegate in the convention, he would personally vote for Wallace. . . . It was at this meeting that Roosevelt told his conferees that he preferred Truman over Wallace, Douglas, or Byrnes, and jotted down the note in longhand which Hannegan was to show me at the convention. . . .

On Thursday afternoon, the day before the Vice-President was to be nominated, Hannegan called me from his room in the Blackstone Hotel and asked me to come to a meeting of the Democratic leaders. When I arrived there, they all began to put pressure on me to allow my name to be presented to the convention, but I continued to resist.

Hannegan had put in a long-distance telephone call to the President, who was in San Diego at the time. When the connection was made, I sat on one of the twin beds, and Hannegan, with the phone, sat on the other. Whenever Roosevelt used the telephone, he always talked in such a strong voice that it was necessary for the listener to hold the receiver away from his ear to avoid being deafened, so I found it possible to hear both ends of the conversation.

"Bob," Roosevelt said, "have you got that fellow lined up yet?"

"No," Bob replied. "He is the contrariest Missouri mule I've ever dealt with."

"Well, you tell him," I heard the President say, "if he wants to break up the Democratic party in the middle of a war, that's his responsibility."

With that, he banged down the phone.

I was completely stunned. I sat for a minute or two and then got up and began walking around the room. All the others were watching me and not saying a word.

"Well," I said finally, "if that is the situation, I'll have to say yes, but why the hell didn't he tell me in the first place?"

From *Memoirs by Harry S. Truman; Volume One, Year of Decisions.* Published by Doubleday & Company, Inc., 1955.

Presidents of the caliber of Jefferson and Lincoln don't tend to reappear, but we had one in the nineteen thirties when Franklin Delano Roosevelt took over. He was a great, great president. He had the ability to make people believe he was right and go along with the things he wanted to do, and he was also very daring in his actions. He surrounded himself with people who were knowledgeable historically about the things that had happened before their time and understood how to use past experiences in current circumstances, and he knew how to make the thinkers of the country work for him. That's always necessary for the head of a government. He must know how to stop the overly radical thinkers before they take over, and he must know how to make use of what they can contribute and use it for the benefit of all the people and not just a few. And Franklin Roosevelt certainly did.

People are always asking me what I thought of Roosevelt as a person, aside from his presidential abilities. Well, I'm sorry I have to disappoint people who love gossip and are hoping I'll have something unpleasant to say, but I liked him. I liked him a lot. He was a very easy person to like because he was a very, very pleasant man and a great conversationalist, with marvelous flashes of humor in almost everything he said, and he had a personality that made people feel close to him. For those reasons, as well as for my tremendous admiration for him as our president, I was very fond of him. And when he died so suddenly and so quickly on April 12, 1945, just sixty-three years of age, I felt truly overwhelming sorrow—not just because he had done so many wonderful things in his administration, and I wanted to see him complete his fourth term and finish the job, but as though I'd lost a close relative or my closest friend.

From *Where the Buck Stops: The Personal and Private Writings of Harry S. Truman*, edited by Margaret Truman. Published by Warner Books, Inc., 1989.

In 1944 the Democratic party was sharply divided. Powerful voices were urging President Roosevelt to drop current vice-president Henry Wallace in favor of a new candidate; among the men suggested was Harry Truman, who had made a name for himself as an honest, intelligent public servant with his work on the Truman Committee. Truman had a variety of reasons for resisting such a suggestion. He wrote to Margaret, "1600 Pennsylvania Avenue is a nice address but I'd rather not move in through the back door—or any other door at sixty." The senator knew that President Roosevelt was gravely ill and likely would not live to complete another term in office; Truman also felt that he, at sixty, was too old to take on the enormous challenge of being president in wartime. And there was another reason for his resistance: Bess. Mrs. Truman had long looked forward to a quiet retirement in Independence. In the end, however, Truman would choose service to his country over all else. ABOVE RIGHT: Truman campaigns in a car with Senator Tom Connally in a parade in Truman's hometown of Lamar, Missouri, September 1944. Photo by Sid Tager. BELOW RIGHT: Truman and Roosevelt ride in an open car with the president's dog, Fala. Photo by The Kansas City *Star*

Diary April 12, 1945

At 3:35 I was presiding over Senate. Senate adjourned about five o'clock and Sam Rayburn called me up and asked me to come over to his office—some legislative matters about which he wanted to talk. I arrived at Rayburn's office about 5:05 and there was a call from Steve Early asking me to come to the White House as quickly as possible. . . . Before going I went to my office, got my hat . . . arrived there about 5:25 P.M., I should say, and was ushered into Mrs. Roosevelt's study on second floor.

Mrs. Roosevelt and Steve Early and Colonel and Mrs. Boettiger were there—Mrs. Roosevelt put her arm around my shoulder and said, "The President is dead." That was the first inkling I had of the seriousness of the situation.

I then asked them what I could do, and she said—"What can we do for you?" . . .

I was very much shocked. I am not easily shocked but was certainly shocked when I was told of the President's death and the weight of the Government had fallen on my shoulders. I did not know what reaction the country would have to the death of a man whom they all practically worshipped. I was worried about the reaction of the Armed Forces. I did not know what effect the situation would have on the war effort, price control, war production, and everything that entered into the emergency that then existed. I knew the President had a great many meetings with Churchill and Stalin. I was not familiar with any of these things and it was really something to think about but I decided the best thing to do was to go home and get as much rest as possible and face the music.

My wife and daughter and mother-in-law were at the apartment of our next door neighbor, and their daughter Mrs. Irving Wright was present. They had had a turkey dinner and they gave us something to eat. I had not had anything to eat since noon. Went to bed, went to sleep, and did not worry any more.

In November of 1944, the American people chose Franklin Delano Roosevelt and his running mate, Harry S. Truman, for their president and vice-president. Truman served fewer than three months as vice-president before FDR finally succumbed to his illness and died on April 12, 1945. In those months Truman had seen the president only two or three times, and he had been kept in the dark about the president's business; most importantly, he had no knowledge of the new atomic weapon being prepared for use in World War II. ABOVE: The flag flies at half-mast above the White House as the nation mourns the death of President Franklin Delano Roosevelt. Roosevelt died at 4:45 P.M. on April 12, 1945, in Warm Springs, Georgia, where he traveled frequently seeking healing for his polio-stricken legs. The president, who was suffering from high blood pressure and arteriosclerosis, died of a cerebral hemorrhage while posing for a portrait. Photo copyright © 1945, The Washington *Post*. Reprinted with permission.

Boys, if you ever pray, pray for me now. I don't know whether you fellows ever had a load of hay fall on you, but when they told me yesterday what had happened, I felt like the moon, the stars, and all the planets had fallen on me.

—HARRY S. TRUMAN
SPEAKING TO REPORTERS AFTER
ROOSEVELT'S DEATH

President Harry Truman, along with James Byrnes and Henry Wallace, met the train carrying FDR's body at Union Station in Washington and rode back in the procession to the White House. Roosevelt's funeral was held in the East Room. At the request of Eleanor Roosevelt, there were no eulogies and Bishop Angus Dun closed the service with the line from Roosevelt's 1933 inaugural address: "Let me assert my firm belief that the only thing we have to fear is fear itself." LEFT: President Franklin Delano Roosevelt's funeral procession makes its way from Union Station to the White House. Photo copyright © 1945, The Washington Post. Reprinted with permission.

Truman was sworn in as president at 7:09 P.M. on April 12, 1945, not quite two and a half hours after the death of President Roosevelt. The oath was sworn over the only Bible readily available, a Gideon taken from the desk of the White House head usher. Shortly thereafter, Truman met with Roosevelt's cabinet and made his first decision as president—the San Francisco conference on the United Nations would go on as Roosevelt had planned. ABOVE: Harry S. Truman takes the oath of office as President. Photo by National Park Services, courtesy Harry S. Truman Library

With great humility, I call upon all Americans to help me keep our nation united in defense of those ideals which have been so eloquently proclaimed by Franklin Roosevelt. I want in turn to assure my fellow Americans and all those who love peace and liberty throughout the world that I will support and defend those ideals with all my strength and all my heart. That is my duty and I shall not shirk it.

All of us are praying for a speedy victory. Every day peace is delayed costs a terrible toll. The armies of liberation are bringing to an end Hitler's ghastly threat to dominate the world. Tokyo rocks under the weight of our bombs. . . . I want the entire world to know that this direction must and will remain—unchanged and unhampered!

Our demand has been, and it remains—Unconditional Surrender.

At this moment I have in my heart a prayer. As I have assumed my duties, I humbly pray almighty God, in the words of King Solomon: Give therefore Thy servant an understanding heart to judge Thy people, that I may discern between good and bad: for who is able to judge this Thy so great a people? I ask only to be a good and faithful servant of my Lord and my people.

—HARRY S. TRUMAN, ADDRESS TO CONGRESS, MONDAY, APRIL 16, 1945

THE BIG THREE AT POTSDAM

BY HARRY S. TRUMAN

've only had one letter from you since I left home. I look carefully through every pouch that comes—but so far not much luck. I had to dictate you one yesterday in order to get it off in the pouch. I told you about Churchill's call and Stalin's calling and staying to lunch.

The first session was yesterday in one of the Kaiser's palaces. I have a private suite in it that is really palatial. The conference room is about forty by sixty and we sit at a large round table—fifteen of us. I have four and they each have four (seats), then behind me are seven or eight more helpers. Stalin moved to make me the presiding officer as soon as we sat down and Churchill agreed.

It makes presiding over the Senate seem tame. The boys say I gave them an earful. I hope so. Admiral Leahy said he'd never seen an abler job and Byrnes and my fellows seemed to be walking on air. I was so scared I didn't know whether things were going according to Hoyle or not. Anyway a start has been made and I've gotten what I came for—Stalin goes to war August 15 with no strings on it. . . . I'll say that we'll end the war a year sooner now, and think of the kids who won't be killed! That is the important thing. . . .

Wish you and Margie were here. But it is a forlorn place and would only make you sad.

From a letter Truman wrote to Bess from Berlin, Germany, on July 18, 1945.

Harry Truman had been president fewer than three months when he sailed on the USS Augusta for Antwerp, Belgium, in July of 1945. From Antwerp, the president flew to Potsdam, Germany, where he was to meet with British Prime Minister Winston Churchill and Russian Premier Joseph Stalin. On these three leaders fell the responsibility for deciding the post-war fate of much of Europe as well as the future of the war with Japan. RIGHT: President Truman has lunch with American servicemen aboard the USS Augusta. The Augusta, carrying the president's personal entourage of more than fifty people, was accompanied by the light cruiser USS Philadelphia. For a man used to making his own travel arrangements, the trip seemed an enormous production. "It seems," Truman wrote to his daughter, "to take two warships to get your pa across the pond." Photo by U.S. Navy, courtesy National Archives

President Franklin Roosevelt, British prime minister Winston Churchill, and Russian premier Joseph Stalin were known during World War II as the "Big Three" in recognition of their positions as the leaders of three of the world's most powerful nations. Roosevelt and Churchill were close friends and their countries natural allies. Their alliance with Stalin was much more tenuous, however, and was based upon a common opposition to Germany and Japan rather than any shared values or vision. By the opening of the Potsdam Conference, the face of the Big Three had changed, with Harry Truman representing the United States; and before the conference was finished, only Stalin remained of the original three. In mid-conference, Winston Churchill returned to England for his nation's elections. He was defeated in his bid for reelection, and it was the new prime minister, Clement Attlee, who returned to complete the meetings at Potsdam. LEFT: Harry Truman stands between Churchill and Stalin on the steps of Churchill's Potsdam residence on July 23, 1945. At Potsdam, Truman, who only months before had been a little-known United States senator from Missouri, stepped confidently into his role as one of the most powerful leaders in the world. Photo by U.S. Army, courtesy Harry S. Truman Library

Your letter of the16th came yesterday and those of the 17th and 19th came this morning. I am most happy to hear from you. I suppose the radio keeps you well informed on my movements.

The conference has met every day since the 17th. Many things have been accomplished and many more which should be accomplished have not been acted upon. But we have time yet to get most of them in some sort of shape for a peace conference.

Stalin gave his state dinner night before last, and it was a wow. Started with caviar and vodka and wound up with watermelon and champagne, with smoked fish, fresh fish, venison, chicken, duck and all sorts of vegetables in between. There was a toast every five minutes until at least twenty-five had been drunk. I ate very little and drank less, but it was a colorful and enjoyable occasion.

When I had Stalin & Churchill here for dinner, I think I told you that a young sergeant named List from Philadelphia played the piano, and a boy from the Metropolitan Orchestra played the the violin. They are the best we have, and they are very good. Stalin sent to Moscow and brought on his two best pianists and two female violinists. They were excellent. Played Chopin, Liszt, Tschaikovsky and all the rest. I congratulated him and them on their ability. . . . It was a nice dinner.

From a letter Truman wrote to his mother and sister from Berlin, Germany, on July 23, 1945.

An Historic Occasion

BY HARRY S. TRUMAN

The following day, July 20, I drove to the United States Group Control Council headquarters in Berlin to participate in the official raising of the Stars and Stripes over Berlin. The ceremonies were held in the courtyard of the buildings which had formerly been the home of the German Air Defense Command for Berlin. Honors were accorded by an Army band and an honor guard from Company E of the 41st Infantry. In the party with me were Secretary Stimson, Assistant Secretary McCloy, and Generals Eisenhower, Bradley, Patton, and Clay.

As the flag was officially raised over the U.S.-controlled section of Berlin—the same flag, incidentally, which had flown over the United States Capitol in Washington when war was declared against Germany and which had been taken to Rome after that city's capture—I made the following remarks:

"General Eisenhower, officers, and men: This is an historic occasion. We have conclusively proved that a free people can successfully look after the affairs of the world. We are here today to raise the flag of victory over the capital of our greatest adversary. In doing this, we must remember that in raising this flag we are raising it in the name of the people of the United States who are looking forward to a better world, a peaceful world, a world in which all the people will have an opportunity to enjoy the good things in life and not just a few at the top. Let's not forget that we are fighting for peace and for the welfare of mankind. We are not fighting for conquest. There is not one piece of territory or one thing of a monetary nature that we want out of this war. We want peace and prosperity for the world as a whole. We want to see the time come when we can do the things in peace that we have been able to do in war. If we can put this tremendous machine of ours, which has made this victory possible, to work for peace, we could look forward to the greatest age in the history of mankind. That is what we propose to do."

From *Memoirs by Harry S. Truman; Volume One, Year of Decisions.* Published by Doubleday & Company, Inc., 1955.

True to his character, Truman worked arduously to prepare for the Potsdam Conference, determined to meet Churchill and Stalin on equal footing. Churchill he found charming, if not too much of a flatterer; eventually the two men would become close friends. Of Stalin, Truman remarked, he is "honest, but smart as hell." It would be many years before Truman came to understand the true nature of the Russian premier. RIGHT: The Big Three and their staffs at the final meeting of the Potsdam Conference. Photo courtesy National Archives

W e—the President of the United States, the President of the National Government of the Republic of China, and the Prime Minister of Great Britain, representing the hundreds of millions of our countrymen, have conferred and agree that Japan shall be given an opportunity to end this war.

The prodigious land, sea and air forces of the United States, the British Empire and of China, many times reinforced by their armies and air fleets from the west, are poised to strike the final blows upon Japan. This military power is sustained and inspired by the determination of all the allied Nations to prosecute the war against Japan until she ceases to resist.

The result of the futile and senseless German resistance to the might of the aroused free peoples of the world stands forth in awful clarity as an example to the people of Japan. The might that now converges on Japan is immeasurably greater than that which, when applied to the resisting Nazis, necessarily laid waste to the lands, the industry and the method of life of the whole German people. The full application of our military power, backed by our resolve, *will* mean the inevitable and complete destruction of the Japanese armed forces and just as inevitably the utter devastation of the Japanese homeland.

The time has come for Japan to decide whether she will continue to be controlled by those self-willed militaristic advisers whose unintelligent calculations have brought the Empire of Japan to the threshold of annihilation, or whether she will follow the path of reason. Following are our terms. We will not deviate from them. There are no alternatives. We shall brook no delay.

There must be eliminated for all time the authority and influence of those who have deceived and misled the people of Japan into embarking on world conquest, for we insist that a new order of peace, security and justice will be impossible until irresponsible militarism is driven from the world.

Until such a new order is established *and* until there is convincing proof that Japan's war-making power is destroyed, points in Japanese territory to be designated by the Allies shall be occupied to secure the achievement of the basic objectives we are here setting forth.

The Japanese military forces, after being completely disarmed, shall be permitted to return to their homes with the opportunity to lead peaceful and productive lives.

We do not intend that the Japanese shall be enslaved as a race or destroyed as a nation, but stern justice shall be meted out to all war criminals, including those who have visited cruelties upon our prisoners. The Japanese Government shall remove all obstacles to the revival and strengthening of democratic tendencies among the Japanese people. Freedom of speech, of religion, and of thought, as well as respect for the fundamental human rights shall be established.

Japan shall be permitted to maintain such industries as will sustain her economy and permit the exaction of just reparations in kind, but not those which would enable her to re-arm for war. To this end, access to, as distinguished from control of, raw materials shall be permitted. Eventual Japanese participation in world trade relations shall be permitted.

The occupying forces of the Allies shall be withdrawn from Japan as soon as these objectives have been accomplished and there has been established in accordance with the freely expressed will of the Japanese people a peacefully inclined and responsible government.

We call upon the government of Japan to proclaim now the unconditional surrender of all Japanese armed forces, and to provide proper and adequate assurances of their good faith in such action. The alternative for Japan is prompt and utter destruction.

The Potsdam Declaration, July 1945.

Diary July 25, 1945
Potsdam

We met at 11 A.M. today. That is Stalin, Churchill, and the U.S. President. But I had a most important session with Lord Mountbatten and General Marshall before that. We have discovered the most terrible bomb in the history of the world. It may be the fire destruction prophesied in the Euphrates Valley Era, after Noah and his fabulous Ark.

Anyway we "think" we have found the way to cause a disintegration of the atom. An experiment in the New Mexican desert was startling—to put it mildly. Thirteen pounds of the explosive caused the complete disintegration of a steel tower 60 feet high, created a crater 6 feet deep and 1,200 feet in diameter, knocked over a steel tower a half mile away and knocked men down 10,000 yards away. The explosion was visible for more than 200 miles and audible for 40 miles and more.

Harry Truman loved the work of a politician. He loved meeting the voters, he loved serving his constituents and his country; yet he was often troubled by the corruption that he saw ruin many good men. "While it looks good from the sidelines to have control and get your name in both papers every day and pictures every other day," he wrote to Bess, "it's not a pleasant position." *RIGHT: Judge Truman talks on the telephone in 1934. Photo by St. Louis* Post Dispatch

Truman announced his candidacy for the United States Senate on May 14, 1934. A successful local politician, but little known outside Jackson County, Truman was given a chance at victory only because of his ties to the powerful Pendergasts. *ABOVE: Truman campaigns below a poster of President Franklin Delano Roosevelt. Photo courtesy Harry S. Truman Library*

BELOW: Judge Truman is joined by his wife Bess and daughter Margaret in December 1934 at the unveiling of a statue of Andrew Jackson outside the new Kansas City courthouse. Earlier that year another courthouse, in Independence, had been dedicated. Its completion was what Truman once called one of the proudest moments of his public life. Photo by Roger Reynolds, The Kansas City Star

ABOVE: Vice-presidential candidate Harry S. Truman and his mother, Martha Truman, at the family's Grandview farm in July of 1944. Mrs. Truman was ninety-one years old at the time. Mistakenly characterized as a naive countrywoman by many, Mrs. Truman was in fact an educated and intelligent woman who followed her son's career with great interest. While Harry was in the Senate, his mother read the Congressional Record daily to keep track of his work in Washington. Photo by The Kansas City Star

LEFT: Truman and Churchill at Potsdam in July 1945. Truman was amused to find that he was in fact taller than the great prime minister from England. Conscious of this fact, Churchill tried always to be standing on a step above when photographed with the American president. Photo courtesy National Archives. Truman's quarters at Potsdam were located at Number 2 Kaiserstrasse. Truman was told at the time that the house had formerly belonged to the head of the Nazi film industry; he learned later that the true owners were a German publisher and his family who were violently removed from their home by the Soviets. BELOW: Churchill, Truman, and Stalin relax in the palace garden before a meeting of the Potsdam Conference. Photo by U.S. Signal Corps, courtesy National Archives

Diary July 16, 1945
Potsdam

Mr. Churchill called by phone last night and said he'd like to call—for me to set the hour. I did—for 11 A.M. this morning. He was on time to the dot. His daughter told Gen. Vaughn he hadn't been up so early in ten years! I'd been up for four and one half hours.

We had a most pleasant conversation. He is a most charming and a very clever person—meaning clever in the English not the Kentucky sense. He gave me a lot of hooey about how great my country is and how he loved Roosevelt and how he intended to love me etc. etc. Well I gave him as cordial a reception as I could—being naturally (I hope) a polite and agreeable person.

I am sure we can get along if he doesn't try to give me too much soft soap. You know soft soap is made of ash hopper lye and it burns to beat hell when it gets into the eyes. It's fine for chigger bites but not so good for rose complexions. But I haven't a rose complexion.

TRUMAN'S FATEFUL DECISION

BY HARRY S. TRUMAN

I was the president who made the decision to unleash that terrible power, of course, and it was a difficult and dreadful decision to have to make. Some people have the mistaken impression that I made it on my own and in haste and almost on impulse, but it was nothing like that at all.

If I live to be a hundred years old, I'll never forget the day I was first told about the atomic bomb. It was about 7:30 P.M. on the evening of April 12, 1945, just hours after Franklin Roosevelt had died at 3:35 P.M., and no more than half an hour after I was sworn in as president at 7:09 P.M. Henry L. Stimson, who was Roosevelt's Secretary of War and then mine, took me aside and reminded me that Roosevelt had authorized the development of a sort of superbomb and that that bomb was almost ready. I was still stunned by Roosevelt's death and by the fact that I was now president, and I didn't think much more about it at the time. But then, on April 26, Stimson asked for a meeting in my office, at which he was joined by Major General Leslie Groves, who was in charge of the operation that was developing the bomb, the Manhattan Project. The meeting was so secret that Groves came into the White House by the back door. And at the meeting, Stimson handed me a memorandum that said, "Within four months we shall in all probability have completed the most terrible weapon ever known in human history, one bomb which could destroy a whole city." . . .

Stimson's memo suggested the formation of a committee to assist me in deciding whether or not to use the bomb on Japan, and I agreed completely. . . . Then, on May 8, my sixty-first birthday, the Germans surrendered, and I had to remind our country that the war was only half over, that we still had to face the war with Japan. The winning of that war, we all knew, might even be more difficult to accomplish, because the Japanese were self-proclaimed fanatic warriors who made it all too clear that they preferred death to defeat in battle. Just a month before, after our soldiers and Marines landed on Okinawa, the Japanese lost 100,000 men out of the 120,000 in their garrison, and yet, though they were defeated without any question in the world, thousands more Japanese soldiers fell on their own grenades and died rather than surrender.

Nevertheless, I pleaded with the Japanese in my speech announcing Germany's surrender, begging them to surrender, too, but was not too surprised when they refused. And on June 18, I met with the Joint Chiefs of Staff to discuss what I hoped would be our final push against the Japanese. We still hadn't decided whether or not to use the atomic bomb, and the chiefs of staff suggested that we plan an attack on Kyushu, the Japanese island on their extreme west, around the beginning of November, and follow up with an attack on the more important island of Honshu. But the statistics that the generals gave me were as frightening as the news of the big bomb. The Chiefs of Staff estimated that the Japanese still had five thousand attack planes, seventeen garrisons on the island of Kyushu alone, and a total of two million men on all of the islands of Japan. General Marshall then estimated that, since the Japanese would unquestionably fight even more fiercely than ever on their own homeland, we would probably lose a quarter of a million men and possibly as many as a half million in taking the two islands. I could not bear this thought, and it led to the decision to use the atomic bomb. . . .

I know the world will never forget that the first bomb was dropped on Hiroshima on August 5, at 7:15 P.M. Washington time, and the second on Nagasaki on August 9. One more plea for surrender had been made to the Japanese on July 29, and was rejected immediately. Then I gave the final order, saying I had no qualms "if millions of lives could be saved." I meant both American and Japanese lives.

The Japanese surrendered five days after the bomb was dropped on Nagasaki, and a number of major Japanese military men and diplomats later confirmed publicly that there would have been no quick surrender without it. For this reason, I made what I believed to be the only possible decision. I said something to this effect in a letter to my sister, Mary: "It was a terrible decision. But I made it. And I made it to save 250,000 boys from the United States, and I'd make it again under similar circumstances." I said the same thing at somewhat greater length in a speech at a university in 1965:

"It was a question of saving hundreds of thousands of American lives. . . . You don't feel normal when you have to plan hundreds of thousands of . . . deaths of American boys who are alive and joking and having fun while you're doing your planning. You break your heart and your head trying to figure out a way to save one life . . . The name given to our invasion plan was Olympic, but I saw nothing godly about the killing of all the people that would be necessary to make that invasion. The casualty estimates called for seven hundred and fifty thousand American casualties—two hundred and fifty thousand killed, five hundred thousand maimed for life. . . . I couldn't worry about what history would say about my personal morality. I made the only decision I ever knew how to make. I did what I thought was right.

From *Where the Buck Stops: The Personal and Private Writings of Harry S. Truman*, edited by Margaret Truman. Published by Warner Books, Inc., 1989.

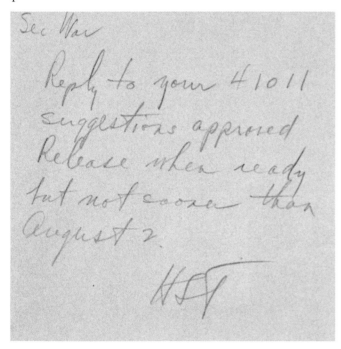

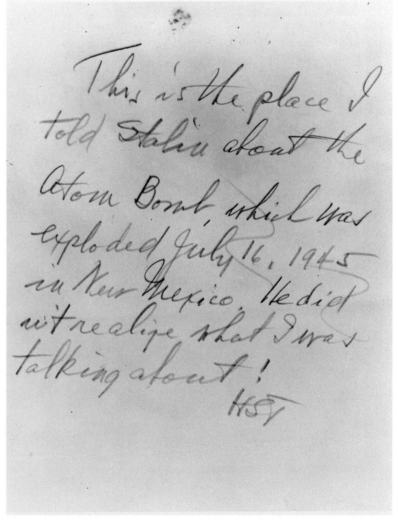

The alternative to using the atomic bomb was operation Olympic, the planned Allied land invasion of Japan. Estimates put the number of men needed for such an invasion at one million; General George Marshall told President Truman to expect close to a quarter of a million Americans to lose their lives fighting on the Japanese home islands. In all of World War II, not a single Japanese unit had surrendered. A land invasion, all agreed, promised victory only after a long, deadly fight. With the full agreement of the Allied leaders gathered at Potsdam, Truman approved the atomic bomb as the best military option. The objective was the surrender of Japan and the end of World War II. RIGHT: Truman made this note on the back of a photo taken at Potsdam. It reads: "This is the place I told Stalin about the Atom Bomb, which was exploded July 16, 1945, in New Mexico. He didn't realize what I was talking about!" ABOVE: The note from president Truman to Secretary of War Stimson authorizing the use of the atomic bomb. Photos courtesy Harry S. Truman Library

UNCONDITIONAL SURRENDER

BY HARRY S. TRUMAN

At 7 P.M. the White House correspondents gathered in my office. Mrs. Truman was with me, and most of the members of the Cabinet were present. I had also asked a former Cabinet member to join me on this momentous occasion. Cordell Hull, now seriously ill and for many years a most distinguished Secretary of State, did not arrive until the conference was nearly over, but I was glad that we could include him in the official picture that was taken of the event. He had done much to make this day possible.

When everybody was in, I stood behind my desk and made this statement:

"I have received this afternoon a message from the Japanese Government in reply to the message forwarded to that government

by the Secretary of State on August eleventh. I deem this reply a full acceptance of the Potsdam Declaration which specifies the unconditional surrender of Japan. In the reply there is no qualification.

"Arrangements are now being made for the formal signing of the surrender terms at the earliest possible moment. . . . General Douglas MacArthur has been appointed the Supreme Allied Commander to receive the Japanese surrender. Great Britain, Russia, and China will be represented by high-ranking officers.

President Truman received news of the Japanese surrender at 4:05 P.M. on Tuesday, August 14, 1945. He made a public announcement at 7:00. Crowds had begun gathering earlier in the day in nearby Lafayette Square; when news of the surrender reached them, they began moving en masse toward the White House. RIGHT: Truman announces the Japanese surrender to gathered reporters. Photo by Stock Montage

"Meantime, the Allied armed forces have been ordered to suspend offensive action.

"The proclamation of V-J Day must wait upon the formal signing of surrender terms by Japan. . . ."

The remainder of the statement was the text of the Japanese note.

The correspondents shouted congratulations as they rushed out the doors to flash the word to their papers. Mrs. Truman and I went out to the fountain on the north lawn. A vast crowd had assembled outside the gates, and when I made a V sign in the manner of Churchill, a great cheer went up. I remained outside only a few minutes and then went back into the White House and called my mother at her home in Grandview, Missouri.

Around 8:00 the crowds outside were still growing, and I went out on the north portico and spoke a few words through a loudspeaker that had been set up there. This was a most significant and dramatic moment, and I felt deeply moved by the excitement, perhaps as much as were the crowds that were celebrating in cities and towns all over the nation.

We had won the war. It was my hope now that the people of Germany and Japan could be rehabilitated under the occupation. The United States, as I had stated at Berlin, wanted no territory, no reparations. Peace and happiness for all countries were the goals toward which we would work, and for which we had fought. No nation in the history of the world had taken such a position in complete victory. No nation with the military power of the United States of America had been so generous to its enemies and so helpful to its friends. Maybe the teachings of the Sermon on the Mount could be put into effect.

From *Memoirs by Harry S. Truman; Volume One, Year of Decisions.* Published by Doubleday & Company, Inc., 1955.

WAR NR2 (VIA WAR) ROUTINE

THE PRESIDENT

MR. CHURCHILL HAS JUST ASKED ME TO FORWARD TO YOU THE FOLLOWING:

"ACCEPT MY PROFOUND CONGRATULATIONS ON THE SURRENDER OF JAPAN

IN RESPONSE TO OUR ULTIMATUM AND UPON VICTORIOUS PEACE."

WINANT.

Mr. Hassett:- Please prepare a nice answer

HST.

Winston Churchill, who had been a close friend and an ardent admirer of President Franklin Delano Roosevelt, found his successor, Harry Truman, a very different man, but a no less capable leader. Churchill called Truman a man of "immense determination" and credited him with helping to preserve the peace and freedom of the world.

Truman had mutual admiration for the British prime minister and often called him one of the great public figures of the twentieth century. ABOVE: President Truman's handwritten note on a telegram expressing Winston Churchill's congratulations on victory, the end of World War II, and peace. Photo courtesy Harry S. Truman Library

VICTORY AND PEACE

BY HARRY S. TRUMAN

The war lords of Japan and the Japanese armed forces have surrendered. They have surrendered unconditionally. Three months after victory in Europe, victory has come in the East.

The cruel war of aggression which Japan started eight years ago to spread the forces of evil over the Pacific has resulted in her total defeat. . . . This day is a new beginning in the history of freedom on this earth.

Our global victory has come from the courage and stamina and spirit of free men and women united in determination to fight. It has come from the massive strength of arms and materials created by peace-loving peoples who knew that unless they won, decency in the world would end. It has come from millions of peaceful citizens all over the world—turned soldiers almost overnight—who showed a ruthless enemy that they were not afraid to fight and to die, and that they knew how to win. It has come with the help of God, who was with us in the early days of adversity and disaster, and who has now brought us to this glorious day of triumph.

Let us give thanks to Him, and remember that we have now dedicated ourselves to follow in His ways to a lasting and just peace and to a better world.

Now, therefore, I, Harry S. Truman, President of the United States of America, do hereby appoint Sunday, August 19, 1945, to be a day of prayer.

I call upon the people of the United States, of all faiths, to unite in offering their thanks to God for the victory we have won, and in praying that He will support and guide us into the paths of peace.

From Truman's declaration of a day of prayer, August 19, 1945, following the Japanese surrender.

My fellow Americans . . . The thoughts and hopes of all America—indeed of all the civilized world—are centered tonight on the battleship *Missouri*. There on that piece of American soil anchored in Tokyo Harbor the Japanese have just officially laid down their arms. They have signed terms of unconditional surrender. . . .

To all of us there comes first a sense of gratitude to Almighty God who sustained us and our Allies in the dark days of grave danger, who made us to grow from weakness into the strongest fighting force in history, and who now has seen us overcome the forces of tyranny that sought to destroy His civilization. . . .

This is a victory of more than arms alone. This is a victory of liberty over tyranny. . . .

Back of it all were the will and spirit and determination of a free people—who know what freedom is, and who know that it is worth whatever price they had to pay to preserve it. . . .

And so on V-J Day, we take renewed faith and pride in our own way of life. We have had our day of rejoicing over this victory. We have had our day of prayer and devotion. Now let us set aside V-J Day as one of renewed consecration to the principles which have made us the strongest nation on earth and which, in this war, we have striven so mightily to preserve. . . .

As President of the United States, I proclaim Sunday, September second, 1945, to be V-J Day—the day of formal surrender by Japan. . . . It is a day which we Americans shall always remember as a day of retribution—as we remember that other day, that day of infamy.

From this day we move forward. We move toward a new era of security at home. With the other United Nations we move toward a new and better world of peace and international goodwill and cooperation.

God's help has brought us to this day of victory. With His help we will attain that peace and prosperity for ourselves and all the world in the years ahead.

From Truman's announcement from the White House to the nation following the surrender ceremony on the USS Missouri.

Within minutes of the announcement of Japan's surrender, the crowds that had been congregating and waiting all day began to move toward the White House, where thousands lined the fence and joined in cheers of "We want Truman!" The president appeared briefly on the lawn with Bess, waved, and then returned inside; continued cheering, however, brought him out onto the porch for an impromptu speech. He proclaimed, "This is a great day, the day we've been waiting for." He then called upon all Americans to help the country maintain the new peace. LEFT: Crowds gather outside the White House after the news of Japan's surrender. Photo by National Park Services, courtesy Harry S. Truman Library

THE TRUMAN DOCTRINE

BY HARRY S. TRUMAN

The drafting of the actual message which I would deliver to the Congress had meanwhile been started in the State department. The first version was not at all to my liking. The writers had filled the speech with all sorts of background data and statistical figures about Greece and made the whole thing sound like an investment prospectus. I returned this draft to Acheson with a note asking for more emphasis on a declaration of general policy. The department's draftsmen then rewrote the speech to include a general policy statement, but it seemed to me half-hearted. The key sentence, for instance, read, "I believe that it should be the policy of the United States . . ." I took my pencil, scratched out "should" and wrote in "must." In several other places I did the same thing. I wanted no hedging in this speech. This was America's answer to the surge of expansion of Communist tyranny. It had to be clear and free of hesitation or double talk.

On Wednesday, March 12, 1947, at one o'clock in the afternoon, I stepped to the rostrum in the hall of the House of Representatives and addressed a joint session of the Congress. I had asked the senators and representatives to meet together so that I might place before them what I believed was an extremely critical situation.

To cope with this situation, I recommended immediate action by Congress. But I also wished to state, for all the world to know, what the position of the United States was in the face of the new totalitarian challenge. This declaration of policy soon began to be referred to as the "Truman Doctrine." This was, I believe, the turning point in America's foreign policy, which now declared that wherever aggression, direct or indirect, threatened the peace, the security of the United States was involved. . . .

After I delivered the speech, the world reaction to it proved that this approach had been the right one. All over the world, voices of approval made themselves heard, while Communists and their fellow travelers struck out at me savagely. The line had been drawn sharply.

> *I BELIEVE THAT IT MUST BE THE POLICY OF THE UNITED STATES TO SUPPORT FREE PEOPLES WHO ARE RESISTING ATTEMPTED SUBJUGATION BY ARMED MINORITIES OR BY OUTSIDE PRESSURES.*

From *Memoirs by Harry S. Truman; Volume Two, Years of Trial and Hope.* Published by Doubleday & Company, Inc., 1956.

At the present moment in world history nearly every nation must choose between alternative ways of life. The choice is too often not a free one.

One way of life is based upon the will of the majority, and is distinguished by free institutions, representative government, free elections, guarantees of individual liberty, freedom of speech and religion, and freedom from political oppression.

The second way of life is based upon the will of a minority forcibly imposed upon the majority. It relies upon terror and oppression, a controlled press and radio, fixed elections, and the suppression of personal freedoms.

I believe that it must be the policy of the United States to support free peoples who are resisting attempted subjugation by armed minorities or by outside pressures.

I believe that we must assist free peoples to work out their own destinies in their own way.

I believe that our help should be primarily through economic and financial aid which is essential to economic stability and orderly political processes. . . .

The seeds of totalitarian regimes are nurtured by misery and want. They spread and grow in the evil soil of poverty and strife. They reach their full growth when the hope of a people for a better life has died.

We must keep that hope alive.

The free peoples of the world look to us for support in maintaining their freedoms.

If we falter in our leadership, we may endanger the peace of the world, and we shall surely endanger the welfare of our own nation.

—HARRY S. TRUMAN, FROM HIS TRUMAN DOCTRINE SPEECH, MARCH 12, 1947

In early 1947, America was enjoying a surge of post-war prosperity. Factories were running again, people were working, incomes were rising—the economy was booming as never before. But the mood of President Truman as he spoke to a joint session of Congress on March 12, 1947, was somber. His specific subject was a proposed $400 million worth of aid to Greece and Turkey, both of which, in a state of post-war confusion, were being threatened by the Soviet regime. Truman's larger subject, however, was the role that the Americans were to play in the post-war world. The president proposed that the U.S. take a stand against Soviet aggression in Greece and Turkey and pledge to maintain a resolute stand against the expansion of communism throughout the world. LEFT: Truman with, from left, General George C. Marshall, James F. Byrnes, and General Henry H. Arnold. Photo by National Park Services, courtesy Harry S. Truman Library

TRUMAN AND
THE MARSHALL PLAN

BY HARRY S. TRUMAN

It was a plan after the Second World War to prevent the kind of thing we had happen in this part of the country after the War Between the States. . . . You can't be vindictive after a war. You have to be generous. You have to help people get back on their feet.

After the Second World War, Europe had suffered the same way we had, and that made me think that we had to help rehabilitate Europe. It had to be rehabilitated by the people who had helped destroy it.

The reports from Europe that I got in the winter and spring of 19 and 47 . . . it's easy to forget, but I doubt if things in Europe had ever been worse, in the Middle Ages maybe but not in modern times. People were starving, and they were cold because there wasn't enough coal, and tuberculosis was breaking out. There had been food riots in France and Italy, everywhere. And as if that wasn't bad enough, that winter turned out to be the coldest in history almost.

And something had to be done. The British were broke; they were pulling out of Greece and Turkey, and they couldn't put up money to help the people on the Continent. The United States had to do it, had to do it all, and the people and the Congress had to be persuaded that it was necessary.

From *Plain Speaking* by Merle Miller, copyright © 1973, 1974 by Merle Miller. Used by permission of The Putnam Publishing Group.

It is logical that the United States should do whatever it is able to do to assist in the return of normal economic health in the world, without which there can be no political stability and no assured peace. Our policy is directed not against any country or doctrine but against hunger, poverty, desperation, and chaos. Its purpose should be the revival of a working economy in the world so as to permit the emergence of political and social conditions in which free institutions can exist. Such assistance must not be on a piecemeal basis as various crises develop. Any assistance that this government may render in the future should provide a cure rather than a mere palliative. Any government that is willing to assist in the task of recovery will find full cooperation . . . on the part of the United States Government. Any government which maneuvers to block the recovery of other countries cannot expect help from us. Furthermore, governments, political parties or groups which seek to perpetuate human misery in order to profit therefrom politically or otherwise will encounter the opposition of the United States. . . . It would be neither fitting nor efficacious for this government to undertake to draw up unilaterally a program designed to place Europe on its feet economically. This is the business of the Europeans. The initiative, I think, must come from Europe. The role of this country should consist of friendly aid in the drafting of a European program and of later support for such a program so far as it may be practical for us to do so.

—SECRETARY OF STATE GEORGE C. MARSHALL, HARVARD UNIVERSITY, JUNE 5, 1947

General Pershing wrote a book I read some time ago, and in it he said that General Marshall, Colonel Marshall then he was, did one of the most remarkable jobs on the entire western front when he was responsible for moving about a million men and God knows how many horses and mules and ammunition from the battlefield at St.-Mihiel to the Meuse-Argonne for the offensive there.

And as you know I was around there at the time. The Germans were caught completely by surprise, and the man responsible for planning and executing that whole thing was Marshall. Pershing said it was one of the most remarkable things of the war.

So Marshall always was the man everybody knew was going to have a wonderful future. No one who worked with him ever doubted it.

So it wasn't any surprise at all when in 1939 Roosevelt made him Chief of Staff of the Army. He was only a brigadier general, wasn't even near the top of the list of brigadiers eligible for promotion, but Roosevelt reached right down there and brought him up, one of the smartest things Roosevelt ever did. Because General Marshall, more than any other man, was responsible for winning that war. At least that's my opinion. . . .

A lot of them [generals] had big parades after the war, a lot of the generals, but there was never a parade for General Marshall, and he deserved it more than all the rest put together.

I gave him a decoration or two [including the Medal of Honor] but there wasn't a decoration anywhere that would have been big enough for General Marshall. . . .

He was the kind of man who always insisted that he be told exactly what was on your mind, and he never failed to tell you exactly what was on his. Always, when I was a Senator and again when I was President. He was one of the men you could count on to be truthful in every way, and when you find somebody like that, you have to hang onto them. You have to hang onto them.

—HARRY S. TRUMAN

From *Plain Speaking* by Merle Miller, copyright © 1973, 1974 by Merle Miller. Reprinted by permission of The Putnam Publishing Group.

Secretary of State George Marshall made public his proposed plan for European recovery after World War II in a speech at Harvard University's commencement on June 5, 1947. The general urged the nations of Europe to meet together, decide upon their needs for recovery from the economic devastation of the war, and then present these ideas to the United States. Marshall, with the support of President Truman, offered the assistance of the American government to all European nations struggling to rebuild after the war. The plan was actually the work of many in the administration, including the president, but Truman always insisted that it be called the Marshall Plan. ABOVE: Secretary of State George C. Marshall walks to the podium before delivering his address to the graduating class at Harvard. Photo courtesy Harry S. Truman Library

Harry Truman once called General George C. Marshall a "tower of strength and common sense." The president was not alone in his respect for General Marshall; the man who became Truman's secretary of state in 1947 was universally admired by Democrats and Republicans alike. Marshall was a career soldier who had fought in World War I and during World War II served as President Roosevelt's chief of staff. He was honest and direct with an almost uncanny ability to understand and command complex situations. And it was a very complex situation that faced General Marshall when he agreed to become Harry Truman's secretary of state and deal with the problem of war-devastated Europe. ABOVE: The president confers in the Oval Office with, from left, George Marshall, Paul Hoffman, and W. Averell Harriman. The Marshall Plan was approved by Congress in April of 1948. Over the next four years the United States poured an estimated seventeen billion dollars of aid into Europe; the result was a revived economy and a flourishing recovery which benefited not just the individual nations, but the entire free world. RIGHT: Truman and Marshall at Washington's National Airport in November of 1947. The secretary of state was preparing to fly to London for the Conference of Foreign Ministers. Photos by National Park Services, courtesy Harry S. Truman Library

LEFT AND BELOW: The Marshall Plan in action. Photos courtesy Harry S. Truman Library

BOTTOM LEFT: The first Marshall Plan ship arrives in Bordeaux, France. The ship, the John H. Quick, *left Galveston, Texas, on April 17, 1948.*
ABOVE: A Missouri mule, brought to Greece as part of the Marshall Plan, works in harness alongside a Greek gray mare. Photos by Economic Cooperation Administration, courtesy Harry S. Truman Library

CAMPAIGN 1948

BY HARRY S. TRUMAN

always knew that from April 1945, until January 1949, what I would really be doing was filling out the fourth term of Roosevelt, who was a great President, but I had some ideas of my own, and in order to carry them out I had to run for reelection and be reelected, and that is exactly what happened.

Of course I didn't say I was going to run for quite some time. It didn't do any harm that I could see to keep people guessing for a while. I knew I'd be able to win, though. I knew that all along. . . . I knew that the people of this coun-

try weren't ready to turn back the clock—not if they were told the truth, they weren't.

The only thing we . . . I had to figure out was how to tell them the truth, in what way, and I decided that, the way I'd always campaigned before was by going around talking to people, shaking their hands when I could, and running for President was no different. The only difference was instead of driving to the various communities where people were, I went by train. But otherwise, it was exactly the same experience. I just got on a train and started across the country to

Truman was given little chance of winning the presidency in 1948. He was dismissed by many as a caretaker president who had filled in ably enough for FDR, but who was not qualified to be elected in his own right. In addition, the Democratic party was split in three. Former vice-president Henry Wallace was running as candidate of the newly formed Progressive Party, and Governor Strom Thurmond was heading up the Dixiecrat ticket. Neither had a true chance at the presidency, but both were draining support away from Truman. Polls throughout the year conceded the election to Republican Thomas Dewey. RIGHT: Truman in California with Elliot Roosevelt, son of FDR. During a June 1948 trip to California, Truman covered 9,500 miles and delivered seventy-three speeches. The crowds were large and enthusiastic and the president at his informal, folksy best.
Photo by Paul E. Wolfe

tell people what was going on. I wanted to talk to them face to face. I knew that they knew that when you get on the television, you're wearing a lot of powder and paint that somebody else has put on your face, and you haven't even combed your own hair.

But when you're standing right there in front of them and talking to them and shaking their hands if it's possible, the people can tell whether you are telling them the facts or not.

I spoke I believe altogether to between fifteen and twenty million people. I met them face to face, and I convinced them, and they voted for me. . . . Another thing about that election, I won it not because of any special oratorical effects or because I had any help from what you call "the Madison Avenue fellas" but by a statement of fact of what had happened in the past and what would happen in the future if the fella that was running against me was elected.

I made three hundred and fifty-two speeches that were on the record and about the same number that were not. I traveled altogether thirty-one thousand seven hundred miles I believe, and it was the last campaign in which that kind of approach was made, and now, of course, everything is television, and the candidates travel from one place to another by jet airplane, and I don't like that.

You get a real feeling of this country and the people in it when you're on a train, speaking from the back of a train, and the further away you get from that, the worse off you are, the worse off the country is. The easier it gets for the stuffed shirts and the counterfeits and the fellas from Madison Avenue to put it over on the people. Those people are more interested in selling the people something than they are in informing them about the issues.

From *Plain Speaking* by Merle Miller, copyright © 1973, 1974 by Merle Miller. Reprinted by permission of The Putnam Publishing Group.

Our government is made up of the people. You are the government, I am only your hired servant. I am the Chief Executive of the greatest nation in the world, the highest honor that can ever come to a man on earth. But I am the servant of the people of the United States. They are not my servants. I can't order you around, or send you to labor camps or have your heads cut off if you don't agree with me politically. . . .

I believe that if we ourselves try to live as we should, and if we continue to work for peace in this world, and as the old Puritan said, "Keep your bullets bright and your powder dry," eventually we will get peace in this world, because that is the only way we can survive with the modern inventions under which we live.

We have got to harness these inventions for the welfare of man, instead of his destruction.

That is what I am interested in. That is what I am working for.

That is much more important than whether I am President of the United States.

—HARRY S. TRUMAN,
CAMPAIGN SPEECH,
SEPTEMBER 26, 1948,
SAN ANTONIO, TEXAS

President Truman delivered the commencement speech and received an honorary degree from the University of California at Berkeley in June of 1948. The visit was his official reason for the trip to California, but in anticipation of the fall presidential election, he turned the trip into a fifteen day, cross-country campaign tour. LEFT: President Truman rides in a motorcade in Berkeley, California, in June of 1948. Photo courtesy Harry S. Truman Library

November 7, 1948

Dear Mary:

I am up at an early hour [3:00 A.M.] because I have to see that Bess takes her medicine at 3:30. She has a very bad cold, sore throat and she can't talk. But you shouldn't say anything about it. For some reason Bess doesn't like being in bed and she resents sympathy, even from her own mother. I'm somewhat the same way.

The reception here was the greatest in the history of this old capital. When the train backed into the station the police band played the ruffles and Hail to the Chief and then people began piling on the train. Barkley and I must have shaken hands with at least five or six hundred—some of them Johnnie come lately boys. I finally put a stop to the handshaking. Barkley, Bess, Margaret and Barkley's daughter, Mrs. Max Truitt, stepped into the big, open seven-passenger car which belongs to the White House fleet. Mr. McGrath tucked himself between Barkley and me. The seat's rather narrow for three—especially three with Barkley. So Barkley and I sat up on the back of the back seat.

There were about 800,000 people on the street between the station and the White House. Said to be the biggest crowd ever out in Washington. Barkley and I made speeches from the front steps of the great white jail and then went to a Cabinet meeting to decide on the first message to the Congress.

I found the White House in one terrible shape. There are scaffolds in the East Room, props in the study, my bedroom, Bess' sitting room, and the Rose Room where you and Mamma stayed. We've had to call off all functions and will move out as soon as I come back from Key West.

It will require at least ten months to tear the old second floor out and put it back. In the meantime I guess we'll live at Blair House across the street. It is a nice place but only half as large—so we have no place to put guests. . . .

Lots of love.

Harry

From the bottom of my heart I thank the people of the United States for their cordiality to me and their interest in the affairs of this great nation and of the world. I trust the people, because when they know the facts, they do the right thing.

—HARRY S. TRUMAN
FROM A RADIO ADDRESS ON THE EVE OF THE 1948 ELECTION

Harry Truman was not impressed by polls. He believed, as he always had, that if he could get his message directly to the people, he could win. On September 17, 1948, Truman began a thirty-three day, nearly thirty-thousand-mile "whistle-stop" campaign. On a special train fitted for the purpose he traveled across the country to the West Coast, then toured the Midwest, and finally made a swing through the Northeast. He made more than three hundred speeches and spoke to an estimated six million people. In small towns across America, huge crowds turned out to see the president, greeting his arrival with cries of "Give 'em hell, Harry!" The president spoke of farming, of his family, of his pioneer ancestors, of his Missouri roots. He introduced Bess and Margaret to great rounds of applause. He met the people face to face, the value of which he had learned long ago while running for judge back in Missouri. The schedule was enough to drive any man to exhaustion, let alone a sixty-four-year-old man who was also keeping up with the responsibilities of the presidency. Truman, however, seemed energized by the experience. In Texas, he made twenty-four stops and gave twenty-five speeches in four days; in Ohio, he gave eleven speeches in eleven stops in just fifteen hours. Truman wrote to his sister of his campaign, "Win, lose, or draw, people will know where I stand." On November 2, 1948, the American people declared where they stood; on that day, Harry S. Truman was elected president of the United States. ABOVE: Harry S. Truman, in the train station in St. Louis, Missouri, holds the November 3, 1948, Chicago Daily Tribune showing the headline "Dewey Defeats Truman." Photo from the collections of the St. Louis Mercantile Library Association

Each period of our national history has had its special challenges. Those that confront us now are as momentous as any in the past. Today marks the beginning not only of a new administration, but of a period that will be eventful, perhaps decisive, for us and for the world.

It may be our lot to experience, and in a large measure to bring about, a major turning point in the long history of the human race. The first half of this century has been marked by unprecedented and brutal attacks on the rights of man, and by the two most frightful wars in history. The supreme need of our time is for men to learn to live together in peace and harmony.

The peoples of the earth face the future with grave uncertainty, composed almost equally of great hopes and great fears. In this time of doubt, they look to the United States as never before for good will, strength, and wise leadership.

It is fitting, therefore, that we take this occasion to proclaim to the world the essential principles of the faith by which we live, and to declare our aims to all peoples.

The American people stand firm in the faith which has inspired this Nation from the beginning. We believe that all men have a right to equal justice under law and equal opportunity to share in the common good. We believe that all men have the right to freedom of thought and expression. We believe that all men are created equal because they are created in the image of God.

From this faith we will not be moved. The American people desire, and are determined to work for, a world in which all nations and all peoples are free to govern themselves as they see fit, and to achieve a decent and satisfying life. Above all else, our people desire, and are determined to work for, peace on earth—a just and lasting peace—based on genuine agreement freely arrived at by equals.

—HARRY S. TRUMAN, INAUGURAL ADDRESS, JANUARY 20, 1949

Truman's inaugural address is considered by many to be his finest speech. It reiterated all that he had established with the Truman Doctrine and presented four defining points for foreign policy during the next four years. First, he pledged continued support for the United Nations; second, a continuance of the Marshall Plan. Truman's third point was the formation of a new alliance of the nations of the North Atlantic; and the fourth, which later became known as his Point Four Program, pledged the innovations of American science and industry to the aid of the world's underdeveloped nations. LEFT: Harry S. Truman speaks to the American people for the first time as their elected president on January 20, 1949. Photo by U.S. Army, courtesy Harry S. Truman Library

The United States and other like-minded nations find themselves directly opposed by a regime with contrary aims and a totally different concept of life.

That regime adheres to a false philosophy which purports to offer freedom, security, and greater opportunity to mankind. Misled by this philosophy, many peoples have sacrificed their liberties only to learn to their sorrow that deceit and mockery, poverty and tyranny, are their reward.

That false philosophy is Communism.

Communism is based on the belief that man is so weak and inadequate that he is unable to govern himself, and therefore requires the rule of strong masters.

Democracy is based on the conviction that man has the moral and intellectual capacity, as well as the inalienable right, to govern himself with reason and justice.

Communism subjects the individual to arrest without lawful cause, punishment without trial, and forced labor as a chattel of the state. It decrees what information he shall receive, what art he shall produce, what leaders he shall follow, and what thoughts he shall think.

Democracy maintains that government is established for the benefit of the individual, and is charged with the responsibility of protecting the rights of the individual and his freedom.

—HARRY S. TRUMAN, INAUGURAL ADDRESS, JANUARY 20, 1949

On the night before his inauguration in January of 1949, Truman attended the Presidential Electors dinner at the Mayflower Hotel in Washington. Truman was in a celebratory mood, but added a serious note when he told the gathered crowd: "I was not in any way elated over the election. . . . I felt only the responsibility, and that is what we are faced with now." BELOW: Truman acknowledges the cheers of the crowd from an open car on a Washington, D.C., street. Behind him is the Mayflower Hotel. Photo courtesy Harry S. Truman Library

I accept with humility the honor which the American people have conferred on me. I accept it with a resolve to do all I can for the welfare of this nation and for the peace of the world.

—HARRY S. TRUMAN, INAUGURAL ADDRESS, JANUARY 20, 1949

THE TRUMAN WHITE HOUSE

BY HARRY S. TRUMAN

RIGHT: The Trumans' 1952 Christmas card with a view of the White House from the East Garden. Photo courtesy Harry S. Truman Library

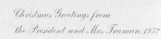

Christmas Greetings from the President and Mrs. Truman, 1952

Diary June 15, 1952

Well here I am, Sunday evening all alone. Margaret came to the great White Prison for the week end on Friday 13th. I went by train to Groton (rhymes with rotten) to speak on atomic energy for peace time use. Should have flown both ways but my staff decided it would be bad weather going up. It wasn't.

The speech was semi political and evidently made a hit. I've never made a speech, since I became President, that didn't have a political flavor. It can't be done.

I've been prowling around the House trying to find my music books which were on the piano at the Blair House. The contractor who remodeled the White House gave me a gold master key to all the Yale locks. It opened all of them tonight but the one I wanted to get into! Just about the time we have things in shape to find what we want, we'll move out and then we'll never find anything. Lesson: Don't raise your boy to be President of the United States.

It is the greatest office in the history of the world. Not one of the great oriental potentates, Roman Emperors, French Kings, Napoleon, Victoria, Queen of Great Britain, Jenghis Khan, Tamerlane, the Mogul Emperors, the great Caliph of Baghdad had half the power and influence that the President of the United States now has. It is a terrifying responsibility. But the responsibility has to be met and the decisions made—right or wrong.

I make them as they come, always prayerfully and hopefully.

Truman envisioned a balcony off the living quarters of the White House as a means of providing private outdoor "breathing space" to him and his family. His plan to add on to the presidents' house, however, brought nothing but criticism from the press, who called him "Back Porch Harry" and argued he had no right to make permanent alterations to the structure of the historic home. But Truman held his ground and got his balcony. The president was reportedly quietly amused in 1948 when the entire East Wing of the White House was found to be structurally weak—except for the Truman Balcony. LEFT: Construction of the Truman balcony on the White House. Photo by UPI/Corbis-Bettmann

When my mother and sister came to Washington at the time I was . . . in the White House, my brother had told my mother that the one bed that was not occupied was the one in the Lincoln Room, and she said, "You tell Harry if he tries to put me in Lincoln's bed, I'll sleep on the floor," and she would have. But I had reserved the Rose Room, which is where the queens and princesses and everybody stay, and I took her back there when she arrived, and my sister was with her. And I said, "Mommy, here's your room." And there was a great four-poster bed that takes a stepladder to get into—it's that high above the floor—and she looked at me and said, "Harry, do you expect me to sleep in that thing? Is that the only bed you've got in this big house?" I said, "No, there's several more."

She went around and looked in the adjoining room where the maid to the queens and princesses and that sort of thing stayed, and there was a nice little single bed in there. She said, "That's where I'll stay," and she did.

She was always a woman who did the right thing, and she taught us, my brother and sister and I, that, too. We were taught that punishment always followed transgression, and where she was concerned, it always did. I was punished, and it hurt, and I tried never to do whatever it was again. They say that isn't the way to do it now, and they may be right. I don't know. All I know is that's the way I was brought up.

From *Plain Speaking* by Merle Miller, copyright © 1973, 1974 by Merle Miller. Reprinted by permission of The Putnam Publishing Group.

Martha Truman, the president's mother, made her first visit to Washington, and her first trip by airplane, in May of 1945. Stepping off the presidential aircraft, The Sacred Cow, she was surprised by the large crowd to greet her and said that if she had known there would be such a fuss over her arrival, she would have stayed home. RIGHT: Martha Young Truman arrives in Washington. Photo by J. Sherrel Lakey, courtesy Harry S. Truman Library. BELOW: President Truman and his mother. Photo by UPI/Corbis-Bettmann

Truman, who loved to travel by train, was the first president to undertake an extended national campaign by rail. *LEFT: The Santa Fe train that carried Truman from Los Angeles to Kansas City in June of 1948. Photo courtesy Harry S. Truman Library*

Blair House, located across the street from the White House, was the Trumans' residence for much of Harry's administration. The day after the election of 1948, President Truman was informed that the East Wing of the White House—the family residence—was in danger of imminent collapse. While renovations were undertaken, the Trumans moved to Blair House, which had problems of its own. Rumors abounded of a large population of rats in the basement, and the hospital located around the corner meant the frequent blare of sirens day and night. The president, however, was little bothered by the move and was happy for the chance to oversee historically correct renovations at the White House. The president's commute to work across Pennsylvania Avenue each morning and afternoon, however, gave the Secret Service added worries. On more than one occasion the chief executive was nearly hit by speeding motorists shocked to see the president in the road before them. *RIGHT: Blair House. Photo courtesy Harry S. Truman Library*

Truman called the presidential vacation quarters at Key West, Florida, the "Little White House"; and he treasured his time there. The nearly three acres upon which the Little White House was located were purchased by the Navy in 1854. The officers' quarters which Truman would one day occupy were built in 1890. RIGHT: The president, Bess, and Margaret are interviewed at Key West. Photo by U.S. Navy, courtesy Harry S. Truman Library

Truman began vacationing at Key West after his physician pronounced him in dire need of relaxation. The submarine base at Key West was the perfect secure location for a presidential retreat. BELOW: The president, Bess, and Margaret in Key West in November of 1951. Photo by U.S. Navy, courtesy Harry S. Truman Library

Margaret Truman, at the age of twenty-four, put her singing career on hold to help her father campaign in the election of 1948. ABOVE: Margaret Truman relaxes on the lawn at the Little White House with President Truman and Bess in November of 1948, just days after the president defeated Thomas Dewey in the national election. Photo by U.S. Navy, courtesy Harry S. Truman Library

Truman spent 175 days in Key West during his presidency and, although these were working vacations, he found the atmosphere a great relief from what he liked to call the "great white jail" in Washington. Bess and Margaret did not join the president at Key West until his fifth visit, after the 1948 election. BELOW: The president and Margaret at Key West. Photo by U.S. Navy, courtesy Harry S. Truman Library

The Key West "uniform" of a brightly colored sport shirt was the invention of a Miami publicist, who sent the president a selection of shirts from one of his clients, the owner of a sportswear store. When photographs of Truman in these shirts were seen across the country, similar shirts began appearing in the mail with regularity. The president soon had so many that he offered them to all his staff and guests at Key West, creating a colorful, recognizable Key West uniform. ABOVE: A selection of the colorful shirts sent to president Truman at Key West. Photo by U.S. Navy, courtesy Harry S. Truman Library

THE WAR IN KOREA

BY HARRY S. TRUMAN

The issue with regard to our Korean policy, however, is not what might have been done, but rather what had to be done. . . .

What we and our allies did about Korea will have a profound influence on the future peace of the world. This was the toughest decision I had to make as President. What we faced in the attack on Korea was the ominous threat of a third world war.

I prayed that there might be some way other than swift military action to meet this communist aggression, for I knew the awful sacrifices in life and suffering it would take to resist it. But there was only one choice facing us and the free world—resistance or capitulation to Communist imperialist military aggression. It was my belief that if this aggression in Korea went unchallenged . . . the world was certain to be plunged into another world war.

This was the same sort of challenge Hitler flaunted in the face of the rest of the world when he crossed the borders of Austria and Czechoslovakia. The free world failed then to meet that challenge, and World War II was the result. This time the free nations—the United Nations—were quick to sense the new danger to world peace. The United Nations was born out of the ashes of two world wars and organized for the very purpose of preventing or dealing with aggression wherever it threatened to break out or actually occurred.

This is why the United Nations responded with such spontaneity and swiftness. This was the first time in the history of the world that there was international machinery to deal with those who would resort to war as a means of imposing their will or their systems on other people.

At the very outset we knew that the United States would have to carry the major burden. That was inevitable because of our geographic position and our strength. Our allies were still rebuilding their shattered nations and binding the slowly healing wounds of their civilian populations. Most of them, too, faced possible aggression by the Communists on their own frontiers.

The Communist aggressors had on several earlier occasions sought to probe what we would do if they moved to conquer and expand. They learned in Iran and Greece and Turkey and in Berlin that we would not be intimidated or bluffed. But up until Korea they had confined their action to subversion, indirect aggression, intimidation, and revolution.

In Korea, however, the world faced a new and bold Communist challenge. Here for the first time since the end of World War II the Communists openly and defiantly embarked upon military force and invasion.

The Communists moved without warning and without excuse. They crossed the 38th parallel of Korea with tanks and planes in open warfare.

We could not stand idly by and allow the Communist imperialists to assume that they were free to go into Korea or elsewhere. This challenge had to be met—and it was met. It had to be met without plunging the world into general war. This was done.

We have learned bitterly and tragically from two calamitous world wars that any other course would lead to yet another world war.

From *Memoirs by Harry S. Truman; Volume Two, Years of Trial and Hope*. Published by Doubleday & Company, Inc., 1956.

Harry Truman considered his decision to send American troops into Korea in 1950 one of the most momentous of his presidency. The conflict that erupted in Korea in that year was, to Truman's mind, an act of aggression against the Republic of Korea by the North Koreans that had implications for the entire world. He understood that the North Korean communist forces' invasion of South Korea in June of 1950 represented an escalation of the Cold War to a new level. The president also understood, however, that such an open and aggressive challenge must be answered with force, yet great caution. Truman's greatest fear during the Korean conflict was another world war; to his mind, with the proliferation of nuclear weapons, such a war would mean the devastation of civilization. Thus President Truman attempted a great balancing act. On the one hand, he refused to accept communist aggression and Soviet expansion. On the other, he tread carefully with the Soviet Union and China lest he provoke either nation into all-out war. At home, the president faced great criticism. He was called weak and indecisive. Yet in his own words, President Truman had "met the test" in Korea. ABOVE: The president at his desk in the Oval Office. Photo courtesy Harry S. Truman Library

FIRING THE GENERAL

BY HARRY S. TRUMAN

I had never underestimated my difficulties with MacArthur, but after the Wake Island meeting I had hoped that he would respect the authority of the President. I tried to place myself in his position, however, and tried to figure out why he was challenging the traditional civilian supremacy in our government.

Certainly his arguments and his proposals had always received full consideration by me and by the Joint Chiefs of Staff. If anything, they—and I—had leaned over backward in our respect for the man's military reputation. But all his statements since November—ever since the Chinese entry into Korea—had the earmarks of a man who performs for the galleries. It was difficult to explain this latest development unless it is assumed that it was of importance to the general to prevent any appearance that the credit for ending the fighting should go elsewhere.

I reflected on the similarities in the situation that had faced Abraham Lincoln in his efforts to deal with General McClellan. Carl Sandburg tells a story about Lincoln's relationship with McClellan: The General occasionally made political statements on matters outside the military field, and someone asked Lincoln what he would reply to McClellan. Lincoln's answer, so the story goes, was this: "Nothing—but it made me think of the man whose horse kicked up and stuck his foot through the stirrup. He said to the horse: 'If you are going to get on, I will get off.'"

Lincoln had had great and continuous trouble with McClellan, though the policy differences in those days were the opposite of mine: Lincoln wanted McClellan to attack, and McClellan would not budge. The general had his own ideas on how the war, and even the country, should be run.

The President would issue direct orders to McClellan, and the general would ignore them. Half the country knew that McClellan had political ambitions, which men in opposition to Lincoln sought to use. Lincoln was patient, for that was his nature, but at long last he was compelled to relieve the Union Army's principal commander. And though I gave this difficulty with MacArthur much wearisome thought, I realized that I would have no other choice myself than to relieve the nation's top field commander.

If there is one basic element in our Constitution, it is civilian control of the military. Policies are to be made by elected political officials, not by generals and admirals. Yet time and again General MacArthur had shown that he was unwilling to accept the policies of the administration. By his repeated public statements he was not only confusing our allies as to the true course of our policies but, in fact, was also setting his policy against the President's.

I have always had, and I have to this day, the greatest respect for General MacArthur, the soldier. Nothing I could do, I knew, could change his stature as one of the outstanding military figures of our time—and I had no desire to diminish his stature. I had hoped, and I had tried to convince him, that the policy he was asked to follow was right. He had disagreed. He had been openly critical. Now, at last, his actions had frustrated a political course decided upon, in conjunction with its allies, by the government he was sworn to serve. If I allowed him to defy the civil authorities in this manner, I myself would be violating my oath to uphold and defend the Constitution.

From *Memoirs by Harry S. Truman; Volume Two, Years of Trial and Hope.* Published by Doubleday & Company, Inc., 1956.

In April 1951, President Truman relieved General Douglas MacArthur of his duties as commander of the United Nations forces in Korea. The response at home was one of shock and vehement disapproval. MacArthur had led U.S. forces to victory in the Pacific during World War II and was considered by Americans to be one of the greatest military leaders in history. Truman, on the contrary, was, in 1951, widely unpopular. Many Americans believed that the president was failing badly in Korea; the public outcry was for all-out war or no war at all. Truman admired the general and trusted his advice on military matters. But the president also believed that the commander-in-chief, not the general in the field, made the final decisions. When MacArthur stated in a letter to congressman Joe Martin that Truman's policy of containment in Korea was wrong, the president could be patient no longer; he called the general home. In the weeks that followed, MacArthur returned to speak to cheering crowds while the president endured repeated calls for impeachment. But Truman never once doubted his decision; and within weeks, the furor over MacArthur's firing had died down and the general had dropped out of public sight. LEFT: Truman and MacArthur meet on Wake Island, in the Pacific, on October 15, 1950, the first and only meeting between the two men. In a conference that lasted fewer than two hours, MacArthur assured Truman that victory in Korea was a foregone conclusion and that there was little chance that the Chinese would enter the war; only later did Truman learn that MacArthur was mistaken in both his assurances. Photo by U.S. Department of State, courtesy Harry S. Truman Library

Dear Mr. Thompson: January 6, 1956

I certainly appreciated your letter of December 29th regarding the MacArthur reaction to my statements in the book.

His blowup was expected, of course, and it seems to be more personal than factual. When an egotist is punctured, a lot of noise and whistling always accompanies the escaping air.

I am not at all worried by what the great general has had to say, and don't let it worry you. If he had stuck to facts, he would be in a much better position. The statements in the book can be supported by the documents themselves, and I fear very much that he understands that and does not really like to see the facts stated. That makes no difference to me, however.

There will be no reply on my part. What is in the book is based entirely on records and facts and my memory—which I think is much better than his.

Sincerely yours,

Harry Truman

Harry S. Truman

In Truman's memoirs, he discussed General MacArthur's dismissal. The president's statements resulted in an angry reply by MacArthur which was published in Life magazine. ABOVE: Truman's letter to Edward K. Thompson, editor of Life.

TRUMAN AND HIS CABINET

BY HARRY S. TRUMAN

Let's take a look, then, at the things I believe a man has to have as president.

First and most important, in my view, is the fact that a president must be strong, particularly when there's the temptation, as there so often is, to look the other way and do nothing because the matter at hand is unpopular or unpleasant or difficult to attempt or accomplish. It may well be true that the best government is the least government, but when it comes to the point where an emergency arises, or when something has to be done . . . then you want somebody in charge who knows how to do the job and can take over and see that things happen. . . .

The ability to make up your mind sounds as if it speaks for itself, but it really isn't as simple as all that. First of all, the president has got to get all the information he can possibly get as to what's best for the most people in the country, and that takes both basic character and self-education. He's not only got to decide what is right according to the principles by which he's been raised and educated, but he also has to be willing to listen to a lot of people, all kinds of people, and find out what effect the decision he's about to make will have on the people. And when he makes up his mind that his decision is correct, he mustn't let himself be moved from that decision under any consideration. He must go through with that program and not be swayed by the pressures that are put on him by people who tell him that his decision is wrong.

From *Where the Buck Stops: The Personal and Private Writings of Harry S. Truman*, edited by Margaret Truman. Published by Warner Books, Inc., 1989.

LEFT: Truman's cabinet, January 1947. From left: Secretary of Agriculture Clinton P. Anderson; Secretary of Labor Lewis Schwellenbach; Secretary of Commerce W. Averell Harriman; Secretary of the Interior J. A. Krug; Postmaster General Robert E. Hannegan; Secretary of War Robert Patterson; Secretary of State George C. Marshall; President Truman; Secretary of the Treasury John W. Snyder; Attorney General Tom Clark; and Secretary of the Navy James Forrestal. Photo by UPI/Corbis-Bettmann

Truman's selection of George C. Marshall as his secretary of state won approval among Democrats and Republicans alike. A career military man, Marshall served as secretary of state from 1947 to 1949 and won the Nobel Peace prize for the Marshall Plan for European recovery after World War II. Marshall resigned his post in 1949 for health reasons but in 1950 came back to the Truman administration as secretary of defense. *LEFT:* Marshall is sworn in as Truman's secretary of state on January 21, 1947, by Chief Justice Vinson. From left to right: John Snyder, Tom C. Clark, Truman, General Walter Smith, Clinton P. Anderson, and Julius Krug. Photo by U.S. Navy, courtesy Harry S. Truman Library. *BELOW LEFT:* General George C. Marshall. Photo courtesy Harry S. Truman Library. *BELOW RIGHT:* Dean Acheson, who was Harry Truman's fourth secretary of state and served from 1949 to 1953, was a major force in the development of Truman's communist containment policy. He also oversaw the implementation of the Marshall Plan and was a key figure in the organization of the North Atlantic Treaty Organization. A tall, refined, Harvard and Yale educated easterner, Acheson was, on the surface, everything that Harry Truman was not. Yet the two men shared a close working relationship and a lasting friendship. Photo courtesy Harry S. Truman Library

HARRY TRUMAN, WORLD LEADER

BY HARRY S. TRUMAN

And now that we have the United Nations, I truly feel that it will succeed if we just give it enough of a chance. I feel this even though, obviously, each nation thinks mostly, and a nation or two entirely, of its own concerns. That attitude isn't very hard to understand, and it isn't so terrible when you stop to think about it. Every member of every nation ought to be proud of his country and spend his time trying to make it the best one on earth. It's no different in this country; there's an esprit de corps that starts in just about every village, every county, every city, and every state. Every citizen of the United States is proud of his state and thinks it's better than any other state in the union, but that doesn't mean that we go to war because we have the same free communications and the same commercial opportunities in every state. And one day, perhaps, we can come to the same conclusion about the world, and if we do, the patriotism toward your home country need never leave you. It can't leave you; it's born in you. It's competition without shooting each other that we're after. That's what we want.

From *Where the Buck Stops: The Personal and Private Writings of Harry S. Truman*, edited by Margaret Truman. Published by Warner Books, Inc., 1989.

At no time in history has there been a more important conference, or a more necessary meeting, than this one in San Francisco which you are opening today.

On behalf of the American people, I extend to you a most hearty welcome.

You members of the conference are to be the architects of the better world. In your hands rests our future. By your labors at this conference we shall know if suffering humanity is to achieve a just and lasting peace.

It is not the purpose of this conference to draft a treaty of peace in the old sense of that term. It is not our assignment to settle specific questions of territories, boundaries, citizenship and reparations.

This conference will devote its energies and its labors exclusively to the single problem of setting up the essential organization to keep the peace. You are to write the fundamental charter.

The essence of our problem here is to provide sensible machinery for the settlement of disputes among nations.

We must build a new world, a far better world—one in which the eternal dignity of man is respected.

As we are about to undertake our heavy duties, we beseech Almighty God to guide us in building a permanent monument to those who gave their lives that this moment might come.

May He lead our steps in His own righteous path of peace.

—HARRY S. TRUMAN, FROM A RADIO SPEECH FROM THE WHITE HOUSE TO THE OPENING OF THE UNITED NATIONS, 8 P.M., APRIL 24, 1945

Our policy will continue to be a policy of recovery, reconstruction, prosperity—and peace with freedom and justice. In its furtherance, we gladly join with all those of like purpose.

The only expansion we are interested in is the expansion of human freedom and the wider enjoyment of the good things of the earth in all countries.

The only prize we covet is the respect and good will of our fellow members of the family of nations. The only realm in which we aspire to eminence exists in the minds of men, where authority is exercised through the qualities of sincerity, compassion and right conduct. . . . I believe the men and women of every part of the globe intensely desire peace and freedom. I believe good people everywhere will not permit their rulers, no matter how powerful they may have made themselves, to lead them to destruction. America has faith in people. It knows that rulers rise and fall, but that the people live on.

—HARRY S. TRUMAN, FROM COMMENCEMENT ADDRESS,
UNIVERSITY OF CALIFORNIA, BERKELEY, 1948

With no experience whatsoever in foreign relations, Truman became president at one of the most tumultuous times in modern history. In seven years and nine months as president, Truman stood at the helm as the U.S. entered a new era in world politics. He led America into the United Nations and then worked with that body to support the creation of Israel and to defend South Korea during the Korean War. The president made a bold statement in support of freedom and democracy with the Truman Doctrine, which promised American aid to any free nation threatened by outside aggressors; and he committed American resources to the Marshall Plan, which helped restore economic stability to post-war Europe. Truman defined the United States' policy of communist containment during the Cold War; in Berlin, he answered a Soviet blockade with the lifesaving Berlin Airlift; and in Korea, his cautious leadership avoided all-out war. *LEFT: President Truman addresses the UN General Assembly on November 24, 1950. On the fifth anniversary of the founding of the UN, Truman told a world-wide radio audience that until there was a disarmament agreement, the world's democracies would continue to arm themselves against the threat of a third world war. Photo by UPI/Corbis-Bettmann*

THE COMMON MAN

BY HARRY S. TRUMAN

Almighty and Everlasting God, Creator of Heaven, Earth, and the Universe:

Help me to be, to think, to act what is right, because it is right; make me truthful, honest, and honorable in all things; make me intellectually honest for the sake of right and honor and without thought of reward to me. Give me the ability to be charitable, forgiving and patient with my fellowmen—help me to understand their motives and their shortcomings— even as Thou understandeth mine!

Amen, Amen, Amen.

The prayer on the other side of this page has been said by me—by Harry S. Truman—from high school days: as window washer, bottle duster, floor scrubber in an Independence, Mo., drugstore, as a timekeeper on a railroad contract gang, as an employee of an untruthful and character assassinating newspaper, as a bank clerk, as a farmer riding a gang plow behind four horses and mules, as a fraternity official learning to say nothing at all if good could not be said of a man, as a public official judging the weaknesses and shortcomings of constituents, and as President of the U.S.A.

You see the thing you have to remember.

When you get to be President,

there are all those things, the honors,

the twenty-one-gun salutes, all those things.

You have to remember it isn't for you.

It's for the Presidency, and you've got

to keep yourself separate from that in your mind.

If you can't keep the two separate,

yourself and the Presidency,

you're in all kinds of trouble.

Had dinner by myself tonight. Worked in the Lee House office until dinnertime.

A butler came in very formally and said "Mr. President, dinner is served." I walk into the dining room in the Blair House. Barnett in tails and white tie brings me a fruit cup. Barnett takes away the empty cup. John brings me a plate, Barnett brings me a tenderloin, John brings me asparagus, Barnett brings me carrots and beets. I have to eat alone and in silence in candle lit room. I ring—Barnett takes the plate and butter plates. John comes in with a napkin and silver crumb tray—there are no crumbs but John has to brush them off the table anyway. Barnett brings me a plate with a finger bowl and doily on it—I remove finger bowl and doily and John puts a glass saucer and a little bowl on the plate. Barnett brings me some chocolate custard. John brings me a demitasse (at home a little cup of coffee—about two good gulps) and my dinner is over. I take a hand bath in the finger bowl and go back to work.

What a life!

From Truman's diary, August 15, 1950.

From Truman's diary, November 1, 1949.

When Harry Truman became president in 1945, the American people, in the midst of a world war and mourning the loss of a beloved leader, wondered how this little-known man from Missouri could lead the nation. The comment was heard on more than one street corner that if Harry Truman could be president, anyone could be president. The "common man" president, as he was called disparagingly, did not have the confidence of the American public. Truman did not dispute his "common man" label. "What," he once asked a reporter, "is wrong with being the average man?" Truman was proud of his Missouri roots, proud of the simple pioneers and farmers who peopled his family tree. He believed in honesty and hard work and in the democratic process that had allowed him to rise from county judge to senator to vice-president and, finally, to the highest office in the land. In time, Americans came to realize that the very qualities that caused them to doubt Truman were those that made him a good leader. He was a humble, plainspoken man of his word, a common man of uncommon integrity, intelligence, and ability. ABOVE: The president meets with the Army and Navy football captains prior to their annual game. Photo by U.S. Navy, courtesy Harry S. Truman Library. ABOVE LEFT: Truman stops during a walk in Marshfield, Missouri, to shake hands with three-year-old Jana Kay Hall in 1952. Photo by AP/Wide World Photos. BELOW LEFT: Truman greets neighbors on his lawn in Independence, December 1948. Photo courtesy Harry S. Truman Library. BELOW: Truman throws out the first ball at a New York ballgame in 1950. Photo courtesy Harry S. Truman Library

CITIZEN TRUMAN

BY HARRY S. TRUMAN

I am not a candidate for nomination by the Democratic Convention.

My first election to public office took place in November 1922. I served two years in the armed forces in World War I, ten years in the Senate, two months and twenty days as Vice-President and President of the Senate. I have been in public service well over thirty years, having been President of the United States almost two complete terms.

Washington, Jefferson, Monroe, Madison, Andrew Jackson and Woodrow Wilson, as well as Calvin Coolidge stood by the precedent of two terms. . . . In my opinion eight years as President is enough and sometimes too much for any man to serve in this capacity. . . .

This is a Republic. The greatest in the history of the world. I want the country to continue as a Republic. Cincinnatus and Washington pointed the way. When Rome forgot Cincinnatus its downfall began. When we forget the examples of such men as Washington, Jefferson, and Andrew Jackson, all of whom could have had a continuation in the office, then we will start down the road to dictatorship and ruin. . . .

Therefore to reestablish that custom, although by a quibble I could say I have only had one term, I am not a candidate and will not accept the nomination for another term.

From a private statement Truman wrote on April 12, 1950. His decision wasn't announced until April 1952.

In 1953, Truman turned over the reins of the American government to Dwight D. Eisenhower and returned with Bess to Independence and the house at 219 North Delaware Street. Truman had declined a run for another term in office. He liked to compare himself to the great Roman leader Cincinnatus who, after serving his country, went back to being a private citizen and a farmer. Truman did not return to the farm, but he did his best to become a private citizen. He had no salary, no pension, and no secret service guards. He refused frequent offers of gifts and consulting fees. When executives from Toyota offered Truman a free car as a symbol of improving relations between the U.S. and Japan, he declined, and then added that he would never drive anything but an American car anyway. RIGHT: In March of 1952 President Harry S. Truman announced to gathered Democrats at a $100-a-plate Jefferson-Jackson Day dinner in Washington, D.C., that he would not seek reelection. His announcement was met by stunned cries of "no, no!" by the crowd. One onlooker, however, was entirely pleased with the news. Bess Truman, seated to the president's right, was thrilled to learn that her husband would be leaving public office behind and returning for good to their home in Independence. Photo by UPI/Corbis-Bettmann

Never gave me any trouble at all. I always kept in mind something that old Ben Franklin said at that meeting in Philadelphia. . . . They had a big discussion about what should be done about ex-Presidents, and Alexander Hamilton I think it was said that it would be a terrible thing to degrade them by putting them back among the common people after they'd had all that power. But old Ben Franklin didn't agree. . . .

[Franklin said:] "In free governments the rulers are the servants and the people their superiors and sovereigns. For the former therefore to return among the latter is not to degrade them but to promote them."

—HARRY S. TRUMAN, ON HOW HE DEALT WITH LEAVING BEHIND THE POMP AND CIRCUMSTANCE OF THE PRESIDENCY. From *Plain Speaking* by Merle Miller, copyright © 1973, 1974 by Merle Miller. Reprinted by permission of Putnam Publishing Group.

I wonder how far Moses would have gone if he'd taken a poll in Egypt? What would Jesus Christ have preached if he had taken a poll in Israel? Where would the Reformation have gone if Martin Luther had taken a poll? It isn't polls or public opinion of the moment that counts. It is right and wrong and leadership—men with fortitude, honesty, and a belief in the right that makes epochs in the history of the world.

—HARRY S. TRUMAN, FROM A DIARY ENTRY, 1945

Cincinnatus knew when and how to lay down his great powers. After he had saved the Republic he went back to his plow and became the good private citizen of his country.

—HARRY S. TRUMAN, FROM A DIARY ENTRY, JULY 8, 1953

Diary January 21, 1953

Three or four thousand people at the station in St. Louis, a grand reception. Crowds at Washington, Hermann, and more than a thousand at Jefferson City, California, Tipton, and all along the line the same. Mr. Younty at Tipton gave me a haircut.

Arrived at Independence one hour late, 8:15 P.M. instead of 7:15 P. M. There were more than 10,000 people at the station—such a crowd and such a jam no one could get through. Never was such a crowd or such a welcome in Independence. There were 5000 more at the house at 219 N. Delaware St. Mrs. T. and I were overcome. It was the pay-off for thirty years of hell and hard work.

I don't recall the date, but it was after Mr. Truman got back from Washington, from being President, and we took a trip down south to Jefferson City. That was on Highway Forty before it was a double-lane highway. And all of a sudden Harry told me to pull over to the side of the road, and there was a woman trying to herd a bunch of hogs that had got loose, and he said, "Let's help that lady get her hogs in."

So I went out and stopped traffic, and he helped her get those hogs off the road. Can you imagine a President of the United States, a former President of the United States, doing a thing like that?

Well, when we got to Jefferson City, there was a reporter there to meet us. Someone on the highway had recognized the President and called Jefferson City saying he'd seen Harry Truman out there herding hogs. The reporter asked him, I don't think he could believe it, thought there was a mistake of some kind, but he asked Harry, and Harry said, yes, he'd done it. He said somebody had to, and he said anyway he'd been a farmer long before he got to be President.

—CAPTAIN MIKE WESTWOOD OF THE INDEPENDENCE POLICE DEPARTMENT, A COMPANION, SOMETIME CHAUFFEUR, AND LONGTIME FRIEND OF MR. TRUMAN. From *Plain Speaking* by Merle Miller, copyright © 1973, 1974 by Merle Miller. Reprinted by permission of Putnam Publishing Group.

A morning walk was part of Harry Truman's routine all of his public life. He recorded his brisk pace in his diary in 1952, "two miles at one hundred and twenty-eight steps per minute." His walks provided time for quiet thinking, and the habit kept him in vigorous health. Truman's walks while president provided a great challenge for the Secret Service agents assigned to guard him, particularly after the 1950 assassination attempt. After his retirement, the greatest threat to his peaceful walks was the constant flow of curious people determined to have a word with the former president. Curiosity seekers cut flowers from his gardens, and fans and critics camped out all night to catch him for a word on his morning walk. Truman understood their curiosity and returned genuine, good-intentioned interest with patience and sincerity. A lifelong student of history, he understood that he, in some respects, belonged to history, and he took this responsibility seriously. ABOVE: Truman walks along a side street in Independence in January 1953. Photo by AP/Wide World Photos. ABOVE LEFT: Truman begins an early morning walk outside his home in Independence in February 1953. Photo by St. Louis Post Dispatch. LEFT: Truman walks with his grandson William Daniel, age five, in Duck Key, Florida, in 1964. Photo by AP/Wide World Photos

Diary July 8, 1953

I went walking this morning as I usually do when the weather permits and my mail reading is not overwhelming.

It was a beautiful sunny morning. I left the backporch where I was reading piles of mail and walked out the gate beyond the old barn—which is now a two car garage. It was a four car garage but these new wide cars have halved its capacity.

As I walked out of the alley into Delaware Street a young man jumped [out] of his car on the west side of the street and said that he and his wife had been waiting for a chance to see me. He was from Strateor (look it up), Ill. , said he'd seen me from the station there on my campaign tour. He was a nice looking man and his wife was a pretty young woman. Both looked sleepy. They'd evidently arisen early so as to be sure they had a chance to see me and shake hands.

I always try to be as pleasant as I can to the numerous people who want to see and talk to me. They, of course, don't know that I walk early to get a chance to think over things and get ready for the work of the day. But they come from every State in the Union and I must consider that they've made a special effort to see me—so I treat them accordingly even [if] it does sometimes spoil a train of thought.

June 28, 1957

To: Mrs. Harry S. Truman
From: H. S. T. No. 38

June 28, 1920	One happy year.
June 28, 1921	Going very well.
June 28, 1922	Broke and in a bad way.
June 28, 1923	Eastern Judge.
	Eating.
June 28, 1924	Daughter 4 mo. old.
June 28, 1925	Out of a job.
June 28, 1926	Still out of a job.
June 28, 1927	President Judge—
	eating again.
June 28, 1928	All going well. Piano.
	Al Smith.
June 28, 1929	Panic, in October.
June 28, 1930	Depression. Still going.
June 28, 1931	Six-year-old daughter.
June 28, 1932	Roads finished.
June 28, 1933	Employment Director.
June 28, 1934	Buildings finished.
	Ran for the Senate.
June 28, 1935	U.S. Senator. Gunston.
June 28, 1936	Resolutions Philadelphia.
	Roosevelt reelected.
June 28, 1937	Grand time in Washington.
June 28, 1938	Very happy time. Margie 14.
June 28, 1939	Named legislation.
June 28, 1940	Senate fight coming.

June 28, 1941	Special Senate Committee.
	Margie wants to sing.
June 28, 1942	Also a happy time.
June 28, 1943	Lots of work.
June 28, 1944	Talk of V. P. Bad business.
June 28, 1945	V.P. & President.
	War End.
June 28, 1946	Margie graduate & singer.
	80th Congress.
June 28, 1947	Marshall Plan & Greece & Turkey.
	A grand time 28th anniversary.
June 28, 1948	A terrible campaign.
	Happy day.
June 28, 1949	President again.
	Another happy day.
June 28, 1950	Korea—a terrible time.
June 28, 1951	Key West—a very happy day.
June 28, 1952	All happy.
	Finish, Jan. 20, 1953.
June 28, 1953	Back home. Lots of Roses.
June 28, 1954	A happy 35th.
June 28, 1955	All cut up but still happy.
June 28, 1956	A great day—more elation.
June 28, 1957	Well here we are again,
	as Harry Jobes would say.

Only 37 to go for the diamond jubilee!

H. S. T.

. . . Your no account partner, who loves you more than ever!

ABOVE: A note written by Harry to Bess on their 38th wedding anniversary. LEFT: Harry and Bess Truman enjoy a Boston versus Kansas City baseball game in 1961. Photo by AP/Wide World Photos

In retirement, Harry and Bess Truman returned home to Independence.

Before they arrived there was much speculation as to where they would live—realtors made offers of beautiful mansions and others suggested luxury apartments in Kansas City; but for the Trumans there was never any question: home would always be the house at 219 North Delaware Street where their courtship had begun more than forty years before. *ABOVE LEFT:* The house in winter. Photo by Vernon Galloway, courtesy Harry S. Truman Library. In retirement, Truman remained as active and hardworking as ever. Devoted to writing his memoirs and overseeing the construction of his presidential library, he also found time for a daily walk, as had been his custom all of his adult life. *ABOVE:* Truman walks in Independence in 1968 at the age of eighty-four. Photo by The Kansas City *Star*

The Trumans returned to Independence by train after the inauguration of President Eisenhower. At the station, nearly ten thousand people waited to greet the former president and his wife and welcome them home. *ABOVE:* Harry and Bess Truman on the porch of their Independence home. Photo courtesy Harry S. Truman Library

Truman began playing piano as a young boy and continued all his life. While he was vice-president, Truman was photographed playing a piano—with the actress Lauren Bacall sitting on top—at a Washington Press Club stage show for servicemen. The photos were widely circulated; as was the rumor that Bess, upon seeing them, forbade her husband to play the piano in public in the future. *LEFT:* The former president plays the piano accompanied by Jack Benny on the violin at the Truman Library in 1959. Photo courtesy Harry S. Truman Library

Bess Truman chose to make the role of first lady a very private one. Nonetheless, according to the Trumans' daughter, Bess had a profound influence on the thinking of her husband; and it was she on whom he relied for advice and guidance throughout his public career. *ABOVE: The Trumans enjoy a quiet evening at their home in Independence, 1960.* Photo courtesy Harry S. Truman Library. *LEFT: The Trumans board a train.* Photo by Harry Barth, courtesy Harry S. Truman Library

Truman shared a close relationship with his only child, daughter Margaret, who was a twenty-one-year-old student at George Washington University when her father became president. Truman often expressed his pleasure at the fact that being the daughter of the president did not change her; she remained, he proudly told friends, the same honest, clear-headed, hard-working woman he and Bess had raised her to be. In 1947 Margaret left the White House to launch a singing career. Although her singing did not always win rave reviews, her father was her most loyal supporter. In 1956, Margaret married Clifton Daniel, Jr.; the couple eventually had four sons: Clifton, William, Harrison, and Thomas. *RIGHT: The former president and Bess enjoy time with their grandsons in 1960.* Photo by New York Times Pictures

A MAN OF INTEGRITY

BY DEAN ACHESON

In his private associations with the people in his administration, he was perhaps the kindest and most patient man in my memory.

But to me his greatest quality as President, as a leader, was his ability to decide. General Marshall, who also had that quality, has said that the ability to make a decision is a great gift, perhaps the greatest gift a man can have. And Mr. Truman had that gift in abundance. When I would come to him with a problem, the only question he ever asked was, "How long have I got?" And he never asked later what would have happened if he had decided differently. I doubt that that ever concerned him. He was not a man who was tortured by second thoughts. Those were luxuries, like self-pity, in which a man in power could not indulge himself. . . .

I have been with Mr. Truman through a great many decisions, foreign policy decisions, decisions about war, peace, whether or not to go through with a difficult, unpopular operation, and never once have I seen him pause to consider whether or not he ought to do something because of its possible effect on his electoral future or the political future of his party. . . .

Mr. Truman may be the most *human* person I have ever known. He is completely without artifice.

Former secretary of state George C. Marshall once stated, "There has never been a decision made under [Truman's] administration . . . that has not been in the best interest of this country. It is not only the courage of these decisions that will live, but the integrity of the man." RIGHT: Truman shows off his casting skills in Sun Valley, Idaho, during his campaign trip in June of 1948. FAR RIGHT: Truman poses in front of the White House during his time as a senator. Photos courtesy Harry S. Truman Library

I t takes a lifetime of the hardest kind of work and study to become a successful politician. A great doctor is known by the size of his practice and his ability as a diagnostician. A great lawyer is known by his knowledge of the law and his ability to win cases and properly advise his clients. A great financier is known by the money he controls.

A great politician is known for the service he renders. He doesn't have to become President or Governor or the head of his city or county to be a great politician. There are mayors of villages, county attorneys, county commissioners or supervisors who render just as great service locally as do the heads of the government.

No young man should go into politics if he wants to get rich or if he expects an adequate reward for his services. An honest public servant can't become rich in politics. He can only attain greatness and satisfaction by service. . . .

I would much rather be an honorable public servant and known as such than to be the richest man in the world.

From a personal memorandum Truman wrote in July of 1954.

Adlai Stevenson once called Harry S. Truman "an example of the ability of this society to yield up, from the most unremarkable origins, the most remarkable men." By the force of his own will, by the coincidences of fate, and by the power of his unswerving faith in God, in himself, and in his country, Harry S. Truman left his mark upon the world. RIGHT: Truman in a Missouri field. BELOW: Truman outside the Grandview farmhouse.
Photos by Bradley Smith

FURTHER READING

Ferrell, Robert. *Dear Bess: The Letters from Harry to Bess Truman, 1910–1959*. Norton, 1983. A collection of the letters written by Harry Truman to his wife, Bess Wallace Truman, from the first year of their courtship through his retirement from public life. The letters reveal the unique character of the former president, as well as pay tribute to the enduring strength of his relationship with his wife.

Ferrell, Robert. *Harry S. Truman and the Modern American Presidency*. Little, Brown, 1983. Truman scholar Robert Ferrell considers the former president's influence on the office of president of the United States.

Ferrell, Robert. *Off the Record: The Private Papers of Harry S. Truman*. Harper and Row, 1980. A collection of Harry Truman's personal papers—diary entries, personal memoranda, and letters—edited by Robert Ferrell. The book covers the years of Truman's presidency, 1945 to 1952.

McCullough, David. *Truman*. Simon and Schuster, 1992. A richly detailed, Pulitzer prize winning biography of the former president, covering his life from childhood in Missouri, through his years as a farmer, a soldier, a local Missouri politician, a United States senator, the vice-president, and president, and also his retirement in Independence, Missouri.

Miller, Merle. *Plain Speaking*. Berkeley Publishing Corporation, 1974. In a series of interviews originally conducted for a television documentary, former president Truman answers questions of subjects ranging from the importance of history, to his relationship with his wife, to his assessment of his own presidency.

Our Presidents, Ideals Publications Incorporated, 1994. A companion to the book *The First Ladies of the White House*, this volume includes a biography of each of the presidents from George Washington to Bill Clinton and is illustrated with formal portraits as well as photographs.

Truman, Harry S. *Memoirs by Harry S. Truman*. Doubleday, 1955, 1956. A two-volume memoir written by Truman during his retirement. The former president describes the experiences of his early life and deals candidly with his public life and presidency.

Truman, Harry S. *Where the Buck Stops: The Personal and Private Writings of Harry S. Truman*, edited by Margaret Truman. Warner Books, 1989. A collection of writings prepared by the former president for publication after his own death, edited and arranged by his daughter, Margaret Truman.

Truman, Margaret. *Bess W. Truman*. G. K. Hall, 1987. Harry and Bess's daughter Margaret presents a loving portrait of her mother, Bess Wallace Truman.

Truman, Margaret. *Harry S. Truman*. Morrow, 1973. Margaret Truman's biography of her father tells his story in the voice of a devoted daughter.

TRACING
HARRY S. TRUMAN'S
STEPS

Harry S. Truman Birthplace State Historic Site, Lamar, Missouri. In the small southern Missouri town of Lamar, the one-and-a-half story frame house where Truman was born and lived for most of his first year is preserved as a monument to the former president. The house was built in 1881 and contains authentic furnishings from that period. It is open to the public seven days a week. (417) 682-2279.

Harry S. Truman Farm Home, 12301 Blue Ridge Boulevard, Grandview, Missouri. Truman lived in this farmhouse from 1906 until 1917. Once a six-hundred-acre farm, today only the nineteenth-century frame house remains. The home contains some of the Truman family's own belongings as well as authentic period furnishings. The farmhouse is open to the public, weekends only, from mid-April through mid-November. (816) 833-1400.

The Harry S. Truman Library and Museum, Route 24 and Delaware Street, Independence, Missouri. Truman himself worked diligently to complete this library, which houses the late president's papers along with a collection of family memorabilia and photographs documenting his life and times. Harry and Bess Truman are buried in the courtyard of the museum. The library is open to the public for study and research. (816) 833-1400.

The Harry S. Truman National Historic Site, 219 North Delaware Street, Independence, Missouri. The home where Bess Truman lived as a young woman, where Harry and Bess Truman lived after they were married in 1919, where their daughter Mary Margaret Truman was born in 1924, and where the former president and first lady spent their retirement is open to the public and contains a collection of the Truman family's personal possessions and furnishings. (816) 254-9929.

The Library of Congress, 10 First Street, Washington, D.C. The largest library in the world, the Library of Congress holds millions of books, manuscripts, documents,

photographs, and prints. Researchers looking to further their knowledge on the life of Harry Truman will find a number of items relating to his life and presidential administration. The library is open to the public seven days a week. (202) 707-5000.

The Little White House, Key West, Florida. Harry S. Truman spent 175 days of his presidency in Key West; he treasured his time there as an escape from the "Great White Jail" in Washington. A museum of Truman's life and presidency is now operated at the site of the Key West Little White House. (305) 294-9911.

The National Archives, College Park, Maryland. The National Archives houses a massive number of photographs and documents of historical interest, including a particularly large collection from the World War II era. The Archives is open to the public for study and research. Call for information on hours and fees, (301) 713-6660.

The National Portrait Gallery, 8th and F Streets NW, Washington, D.C. As part of its extensive collection of paintings, sculptures, and photographs of great American men and women, the National Portrait Gallery includes the Hall of Presidents, which features portraits of every president from George Washington to the current chief executive. The gallery is open to the public free of charge daily. (202) 357-2700.

The White House, 1600 Pennsylvania Avenue, Washington, D.C. Tours of the presidents' home are available year round and admission is free. Call (202) 456-7041 for details on hours of operation and tickets. *Blair House,* where the Trumans lived while White House renovations and repairs were in progress, is also located on Pennsylvania Avenue. The house is not open to the public, but a plaque outside marks the location of the attempted assassination of President Truman and serves as a memorial to the guard who lost his life protecting the president.

INDEX